I0102804

Anonymous

United States Patents, Designs, Trade Marks and Copyrights

Anonymous

United States Patents, Designs, Trade Marks and Copyrights

ISBN/EAN: 9783337407353

Printed in Europe, USA, Canada, Australia, Japan

Cover: Foto ©Suzi / pixelio.de

More available books at **www.hansebooks.com**

New York Cable Address : " Richpatent, Newyork."
Washington Cable Address : " Richards, Washington."

STRICTLY PRIVATE.—FOR PATENT AGENTS AND SOLICITORS ONLY.

UNITED STATES

PATENTS, DESIGNS,

TRADE MARKS AND COPYRIGHTS.

New York Cable Address : " Richpatent, Newyork."
Washington Cable Address : " Richards, Washington."

———

STRICTLY PRIVATE.—FOR PATENT AGENTS AND SOLICITORS ONLY.

UNITED STATES

PATENTS, DESIGNS,

TRADE MARKS AND COPYRIGHTS.

WE TRANSACT BUSINESS SOLELY AND EXCLUSIVELY FOR PATENT AGENTS AND SOLICITORS.

TO PATENT AGENTS.

We take pleasure in offering to our foreign correspondents this little book on United States Patents, Designs, Trade Marks, Labels, Prints, and Copyrights. We have endeavored to present in it a very brief but fairly complete statement of the law and practice in the United States, as it exists to-day upon these subjects, and in such a manner that the busy Patent Agent and Solicitor may readily avail himself of such information as it contains, and make it of practical assistance to him in the daily prosecution of his business.

We are well aware that it leaves much to be desired, and that it might be improved upon in very many particulars. We cannot, however, at present take the time to prepare the more complete and ambitious work that we may, perhaps, publish in the future, and, as we cannot wholly fail to respond to the many demands received for a hand-book of this kind, we offer this in the hope that it may be of some little service to the profession.

Yours very truly,

RICHARDS & CO.

New York, Feb. 1, 1892.

UNITED STATES PATENTS.

WHO MAY BE PATENTEE.

There are absolutely no restrictions whatever as to citizenship or nationality, age or sex. The applicant must, however, be one of the following persons :

(a) The true and first inventor, meaning the actual inventor or discoverer of the thing invented, or

(b) The executor or administrator of a deceased inventor.

A patent may be issued to the assignee of the true and first inventor, but in this case all the application papers *must* be signed by the *actual inventor*, and an assignment recorded before the issue of the patent, containing a request that the Commissioner of Patents issue the patent, when granted, to the assignee. In *no case* is the assignee entitled to make application in his own name.

Joint inventors may obtain a joint patent ; neither may apply for and obtain a patent separately.

Patents may be issued to an inventor and his assignees jointly, by filing an assignment before the issue of the patent, containing a request to this effect.

In case of the death of an inventor between the filing of an application and the issue of the patent, the patent will be issued to the legal representatives of such deceased inventor.

IMPORTERS.—A mere importer, even though the true and first importer is not entitled to apply for a patent.

PATENTABILITY OF INVENTIONS.

Under the law there are eight requisites as to patentability. These may be briefly enumerated as follows :

(a) An invention or discovery must actually have been made, and the applicant must be the true and first inventor thereof, or, in case of a deceased inventor, the legal representative of such inventor.

(b) The thing invented must be new and useful.

(c) The invention must be either an art (which includes a method or process, whether chemical or mechanical), a machine, manufacture, composition of matter, or a new and useful improvement of either.

(d) The thing invented must not have been known or used by others in this country before the applicant's invention thereof.

(e) It must not have been patented or described in any printed publication in this or any foreign country before the applicant's invention or discovery thereof.

(f) The invention must not have been in public use or on sale in the United States for more than two years prior to the application for patent therefor.

(g) The invention must not have been abandoned to public use by the inventor ; *i. e.,* when it can be proven that an inventor, after his invention is perfected, has acquiesced in its use by the public, and by such acquiescence abandoned his invention, concluding not to patent it, but to dedicate it to the public, he cannot afterward recall such abandonment by a subsequent application for patent.

(h) The inventor must file a formal application for patent, and pay the fees prescribed by law.

PATENTS FOR INVENTIONS ALREADY PATENTED ABROAD.

Patents may be procured for inventions already patented abroad, *at any time thereafter*, so long as the invention has not been in public use or on sale in the United States for more than two years prior to the filing of the application. The American patent need not, in such case, be restricted to the precise matter covered by the foreign patent, it may be made as broad as the actual invention. A foreign inventor may obtain a perfectly valid American patent even though his foreign patent is void. (See, however, " Limitation of Term by Foreign Patent)."

DATE, TERM, AND EXTENT OF PATENT.

The patent dates from the day of its *issue ;* is granted for a term of seventeen years (subject to the limitations set forth in the next section) ; and gives the exclusive right to make, use, and vend the invention or discovery throughout all the United States and the territories thereof. The term of a patent cannot be extended except by way of a special act of Congress. Such extensions are costly, and are seldom or never granted.

LIMITATION OF TERM BY PRIOR FOREIGN PATENT.

Every patent granted for an invention which has been previously patented by the same inventor, or by another person with his knowledge or consent, in a foreign country, will be so limited as to expire at the same time with the foreign patent ; or, if there be more than one, at the same time with the one having the shortest unexpired term ; but in no case will it be in force more than seventeen years. An American patent is not, however, so limited by a foreign patent unless the foreign patent was taken out by the applicant for the American patent, or with his knowledge or consent, and further, the inventions must be identical, and the foreign patent claim as well as describe the same invention. It should be noted however, that it has been held by the Courts that an invention covered by a domestic patent is the same as that covered by a foreign patent when the principle is the same, though it may have been improved ; and that a foreign patent limits the American whether it be an open or a secret patent.

To have a limiting effect the foreign patent must actually have been in force or published as a patent before the issue of the American patent. It has been decided by the Courts that no English patent is complete until the complete specification has been enrolled ; that an English provisional specification is not a patent, and that this enactment does not apply to a case where a foreign patent is dated before the issue of the corresponding United States patent but not sealed nor published until afterwards, although it does apply to cases where the United States patent is granted after the foreign patent is sealed, upon an application filed before that event.

Prior to the year 1889 it was held that a United States patent would expire with a prior foreign patent granted for a shorter term, even though the latter should be prolonged, but up to this time this important question had never been passed upon by the Supreme Court. This Court, the Court of final jurisdiction in this country, has now decided (Bate Refrigerator Co. *v* Hammond *et al*, 46, O. G. 689) that in case of a foreign patent granted for a term less than the maximum term allowed by law, but extended by one or more extensions to the full term, that when the statute under which the extensions are granted is in force when the United States patent is issued, and also when the foreign patent is applied for, and when by that statute the extension of the patent is a matter entirely of right, at the option of the patentee, on his payment of a required fee, and when the term of the foreign patent so extended is continuous and uninterrupted, that the United States patent will not expire at the expiration of the term for which the foreign patent was originally granted, but that it will live so long as the foreign patent continues to exist,—not however to exceed seventeen years at most.

It has also been decided that there is nothing in the statute which admits of the view that the duration of the United States patent is to be limited by any lapsing or forfeiture of any portion of the term of a foreign patent by the non-observance of a condition subsequent, or the happening of a subsequent condition, imposed by the statute of the country granting such foreign patent,—such for example, as the failure to pay a tax, or to work the invention.

THE APPLICATION.

DOCUMENTS REQUIRED.

A complete application is composed of the following parts:—

     (*A.*) Petition (with Power of Attorney if an attorney is appointed).
     (*B.*) Specification, with claims.
     (*C.*) Oath.
     (*D.*) Drawings (a drawing must be furnished if the invention can possibly be illustrated).
     (*E.*) A model or specimen, if required.

The petition, power of attorney, specification, and oath must be in the English language. All documents, except the drawing, are required to be written or printed, *on one side only*, of good, strong, white paper, leaving a wide margin (preferably about two inches), upon the left hand of the page.

NO EXAMINATION UNTIL COMPLETE APPLICATION FILED.

An application for patent will not be placed upon the files for examination until all its parts, except the model or specimens, when required, are received by the Patent Office, and all applications filed in an incomplete state, must be completed and prepared for examination within two years after the filing of the petition, or they will be regarded as abandoned, unless it can be shown to the satisfaction of the Commissioner that such delay was unavoidable.

EXECUTION OF DOCUMENTS.

All documents except the drawing, must be signed by the inventor himself if he be alive. He cannot delegate to another by power of attorney or otherwise, the power to sign the documents for him, or in his stead. If the inventor be dead, these documents must be signed by the executor or administrator of such deceased inventor.

EXECUTION IN BLANK NOT PERMISSABLE.

We desire to particularly call the attention of our correspondents to the following rule of the Patent Office, (Rule 31—1891).

" Every application signed or sworn to in blank, or without actual inspection by the applicant of the petition and specification, and every application altered or partly filled up after being signed or sworn to, will be stricken from the files."

It has been a somewhat general practice for patent agents in this country to receive from agents resident abroad, the petition, power of attorney, and oath, signed in blank, with a specification in a foreign language, and then to fill in such blanks, making and filing a translation of the specification sent. It will be seen from the above rule that this practice is indefensible, and that the proper procedure, if the foreign agent cannot prepare the documents in English himself, is to forward a draft of the specifications, and have the translation made before the inventor signs any of the papers. The translated specification, with the petition, power of attorney, and oath, properly filled out, can then be returned ready for execution by the inventor. The Commissioner of Patents has decided in a case where the specification was forwarded to an American agent, already prepared in the English language, but where the agent, on account of numerous interlineations and clerical errors, prepared and filed a corrected but exact, clean copy of the same, that such substitution was a clear violation of the rule, and that he should have filed the copy that was actually sworn to by the inventor, and filed a clean copy afterward, as a substitute specification, if he so desired. It makes no difference whether the inventor can understand the English language or not; he must swear to the specification filed, and that he believes himself to be the original and first inventor of the invention described therein. If he does not read English, the contents of the specification should be made known to him before he executes the documents.

(A.) THE PETITION (AND POWER OF ATTORNEY).

The petition must:—

(1.) be addressed to the Commissioner of Patents,

(2.) must state the name and residence of the petitioner,

(3.) must designate by title the invention sought to be patented,

(4.) must contain a reference to the specification for a full disclosure of such invention, and

(5.) must be signed by the applicant.

(6.) POWER OF ATTORNEY :—While the power of attorney is not one of the essential parts of an application as required by the Patent Office, as an inventor may, if he chooses, prosecute his own application, yet, as a matter of fact, it may be considered as an essential feature, as, owing to the intricacy of the practice in the United States Patent Office, few, if any, inventors have the requisite experience to prosecute their own applications. The power of attorney may be either a separate document or it may be incorporated with the petition, usually and preferably it is so incorporated. It should, however, in either case give the following powers:—

(a.) an appointment of attorney with full power of substitution and revocation, to prosecute the application,

(b.) to make alterations and amendments therein,

(c.) to sign the drawings,

(d.) to receive the patent, and

(e.) to transact all business in the Patent Office connected therewith.

The rules require that a power of attorney given to a firm or copartnership shall name the individual members thereof. Before any attorney, original or associate, will be allowed to inspect papers or take action of any kind with respect to an application, his power of attorney must be filed.

(B.) THE SPECIFICATION, AND CLAIMS.

THE SPECIFICATION is a written description of the invention, and must be in such clear, full, and exact terms that any person skilled in the art or science to which the invention relates, may make, construct, compound and use the same. It must set forth the invention in such manner as to clearly distinguish it from other inventions and from everything that is old and well known ; it must explain the principle of the invention, and the best mode in which the applicant has contemplated applying that principle.

IF THE INVENTION RELATES TO A MACHINE the specification must clearly set forth the exact construction and operation of every part thereof, and of the machine as a whole.

IF THE INVENTION RELATES TO AN ART OR PROCESS the specification must describe such art or process step by step, or act by act, clearly and precisely, and the operation of the art or process as a whole.

IF THE INVENTION RELATES TO A COMPOSITION OF MATTER the specification must enumerate the different materials entering into such composition, the proportions of each, the manner of combining them, and the essential qualities of the resulting combination.

IF THE INVENTION RELATES TO A NEW ARTICLE OF MANUFACTURE the specification must clearly describe such new product and the manner in which it is constructed.

IF THE INVENTION RELATES TO AN IMPROVEMENT the specification must particularly point out in what the improvement consists, and must by explicit language distinguish between what is old and what is claimed as new.

The specification must conclude with a specific and distinct claim or claims of that which the applicant regards as his invention.

When there are drawings the description must refer to the different views by figures, and to the different parts by letters or numerals (preferably the latter).

ORDER OF ARRANGEMENT.—The following order of arrangement should be observed in framing the specification :

(a) Preamble stating the name and residence of the applicant, the title of the invention, and, if the invention has been patented in any country, the country or countries in which it has been so patented, and the date and number of each patent.

(b) A general statement of the object and nature of the invention.

(c) A brief description of each figure of the drawings (if there are drawings).

(d) A detailed description (specification) of the invention.

(e) The claim or claims.

(f) Signature of inventor.

(g) Signatures of two witnesses.

The specification must be signed by the actual inventor if he be alive, if he be dead by his executor or administrator, and the signature must be attested by two witnesses. All names should be signed in full and legibly written.

THE CLAIM.—The office of the claim is to define the exact limits of the invention, and it is therefore the life of the patent so far as the inventor is concerned, for the thing patented is the thing claimed, and no more, whatever the patentee may suppose or assert that he has invented, or even if the thing claimed be less than the real invention.

The importance of the claims, and the necessity that they shall be drawn as broad as the actual invention will be apparent.

GENERAL REMARKS CONCERNING CLAIMS.—Every claim must set forth some art or instrument complete in itself, and capable of practical use. It must be for an operative means, and must state a concrete invention, not an abstraction. It must not cover a principle, nor be for the use of a natural force for a special purpose, although the special method of using it for such a purpose may properly be claimed. General truths and forces belong to all men and cannot be claimed. The claim must indicate the class of patentable inventions to which the claimed invention belongs ; must precisely define it, and clearly distinguish the exact features of novelty. It must correspond with the specification and drawings, and the invention claimed must be identical with the invention described. It cannot cover means substantially different from those described, even though they produce substantially the same result.

In framing claims every element claimed must be clearly stated, not merely inferred, for vague claims are not allowable, and ambiguous claims are void and of no effect.

Indefinite expressions such as " means," " mechanism," " connections," etc., should not usually be used, although their use may be proper when used to denote appliances which are not essential parts of the invention.

FUNCTIONAL CLAIMS.—A claim for an effect or function cannot be allowed. The means by which the effect is produced or the function performed must be specified, and the claim must be either for the physical structure, the combination of devices, or the method of operation.

ALTERNATIVE CLAIMS are not usually allowable. A patentee cannot claim an alternative combination if the separate combinations will not each make an operative machine. A claim to only one or the other of two things, but to neither positively, is void.

EQUIVALENTS should not be expressly claimed, for a claim covers all equivalents even though the inventor never thought of them.

BUT ONE INVENTION MAY BE CLAIMED IN A SINGLE APPLICATION.—The claim must be confined to some single and distinct invention. The general rule is that every art or instrument complete in itself and capable of separate use constitutes a distinct invention, and should be the subject matter of a separate application for patent. It follows therefore that a process and its product, unless the one is absolutely dependent upon the other, and inseparable in their nature, cannot be joined in a single application. A machine and its product cannot both be claimed in a single application if they are capable of use separately. If an article is not necessarily the result of the action of a machine, the applications for patents for the article and machine should be separate.

A claim for a generic invention may however, be joined in a single application with a claim for one species; but if more than one species are to be claimed, a separate application must be filed for each additional species or modification.

Where several inventions are united to form one operative whole and *are dependent* upon each other, they may be claimed in one application. If they are not dependent upon each other and are capable of separate use, or can be used in another art or instrument, a separate application should be filed for each distinct invention.

THE CLAIM FOR A COMBINATION must embrace specifically all of the essential elements necessary to produce a distinct and operative combination, and must at the same time be confined to the precise features of the invention that the inventor has created and described. Features not essential to the combination should not be introduced into the claim, for a claim that includes an element not co-acting as part of the combination is invalid. A claim for a combination should not include the connecting mechanism unless it is an element in the combination or is essential to the comprehension of what is claimed. Each of the elements and sub-combinations, if new and patentable may be separately claimed as well as the combination as a whole.

THE CLAIM FOR AN ART OR PROCESS, should enumerate each of the acts or steps of the process in the order in which they are employed, and should set them forth in such a manner as to identify them with the acts or steps described in the specification. A general claim for a process covers all ways of performing it, and if its elements possess equivalents, a general claim may cover it under all forms. Each step of a process, if a true sub-process, and a complete invention in itself, may also be covered by a separate claim, which may be joined in the same application with the claim for the art or process as a whole.

THE CLAIM FOR A MACHINE must be drawn to cover a specific piece of mechanism or apparatus. It must not be so drawn as to claim a mode of operation, a principle, an idea, a means of producing an effect, or an effect produced. If an invention does not embrace an entire machine, the parts invented must be distinctly claimed. Each subordinate piece of mechanism may be claimed, if new and patentable, even though it is not capable of use in any other connection.

THE CLAIM FOR A COMPOSITION OF MATTER. A composition of matter requires but a single claim, and in this the invention should be set forth by enumerating its elements, the mode of combination, and the essential qualities of the resulting combination. The claim need not set forth the precise proportions in which the ingredients are used, these may and must be set forth in the specification, but where the composition is formed of specific, known ingredients, the claim should mention all of them.

THE CLAIM FOR A MANUFACTURE. A manufacture must be claimed as a new product, and must be claimed independently of the process of making it. It should be claimed by setting forth its essential qualities, and the mode of making it. The words "article of manufacture" have no particular significance or value in a claim, and neither aid nor impair its validity.

THE CLAIM FOR AN IMPROVEMENT upon a known art or machine must clearly state the exact improvement made, and must distinguish the new from the old. It is not sufficient that persons skilled in the art can distinguish the improvement from the original invention, the claim itself must show it.

DEFECTIVE CLAIMS.—A patent may be valid in part if not as a whole. A claim is defective when it fails to completely and exactly define the invention, and is void when it claims more than belongs to the invention. An incomplete or defective claim may be cured by re-issue (see " Re-issues "), and an excessive claim may be cured either by a re-issue or a disclaimer. (See " Disclaimers "). Where several claims exist, the presence of a void claim does not affect the validity of those that are good, unless there has been an evident intention to mislead the public, or an unreasonable delay in curing the defects.

(C.) THE OATH.

The applicant must make oath (or affirmation) to the following facts :

(*a*) That he verily believes himself to be the original, first and sole inventor (or in case of joint inventors, the original, first, and joint inventors) of the invention described in the specification.

(*b*) That the same has not been patented to him, or to others with his knowledge or consent in any country, or, if it has been patented, he must state under oath the countries in which it has been patented, and give the number and date of each patent.

(*c*) That the same has not to his knowledge been in public use or on sale in the United States for more than two years prior to this application, and

(*d*) That he does not know and does not believe that the same was ever known or used prior to his invention thereof.

The oath must also state :

(*e*) The full name and residence of the inventor, and

(*f*) Of what country he is a citizen or subject.

If the inventor be dead, the oath will be made by the administrator or executor, who will declare his belief that the party named as inventor was the original and first inventor, and the form of the oath will be changed to agree with the facts.

EXECUTION OF OATH.—The oath must be signed by the applicant. It may be made before any minister, charge d'affaires, consul, or commercial agent holding commission under the Government of the United States, or before any notary public of the foreign country in which the applicant may be.

The oath *must* be attested in all cases by the proper official seal of the officer before whom the oath or affirmation is made. When such officer is not provided with a seal his official character must be established by competent evidence, as by a certificate from a clerk of a court of record, or other proper officer having a seal.

ADDITIONAL OR SUPPLEMENTARY OATHS REQUIRED IN CERTAIN CASES.—An additional or supplemental oath will be required in certain cases, such as the following :

(1) The Commissioner may require an additional oath if the application has not been filed within a reasonable time after the execution of the original oath.

(2) To cure any defects in the original oath, such as the omission of the declaration as to foreign patents.

(3) If the applicant seeks to introduce, by amendment, any claim not substantially embraced in the statement of invention and claims originally presented, and therefore not covered by the original oath, he will be required to file a supplemental oath to the effect that the subject matter of the proposed amendment was part of his invention, and was invented before he filed his original application.

(D.) DRAWINGS.

The applicant is required by law to furnish a drawing of his invention whenever the nature of the invention is such that it can be illustrated by a drawing. The applicant is not permitted to elect whether he will furnish a drawing or not.

The drawing must show every feature of the invention covered by the claims, and must be so full and clear that, if the invention is a simple one, no model will be needed. The drawings must also correspond in all essential points with the specification.

When the invention consists of an improvement on an old machine, the drawing must exhibit, in one or more views, the machine itself, disconnected from the old structure, and also, in another view, so much only of the old structure as will suffice to show the connection of the invention therewith.

RULES.

The following rules are rigidly enforced, and any departure from them will be certain to cause the rejection of the drawings, and delay the prosecution of the application.

PAPER AND SIZE.—All drawings must be made upon pure white paper of a thickness corresponding to three-sheet Bristol board. The surface of the paper must be calendered and smooth.

The size of the sheets must be exactly 10 inches (25.4 cm.) wide by 15 inches (38.1 cm.) long (high). As many sheets may be used as may be necessary to show the invention fully, but the number of sheets must never be more than is absolutely necessary. Under the present practice, no drawing will be admitted, even for the purpose of examination, unless the sheet is of the correct size.

MARGINAL LINES AND SPACE FOR HEADING.—A single marginal line must be drawn, all around, exactly one inch (2.55 cm.) from the edge of the sheet. One of the shorter sides of the sheet is regarded as its top, and measuring downwardly from the marginal line, a clear

(A clear space of 1¼ inches must be left here for the Heading
and Title that is inserted by the Patent Office.)

Fig. 2.

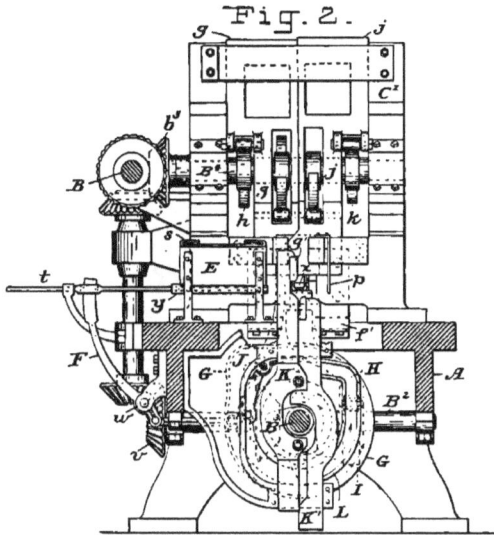

Fig. 3.

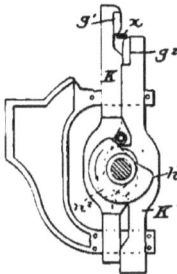

Fig. 4.

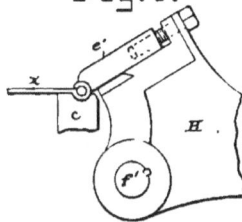

Fig. 5.

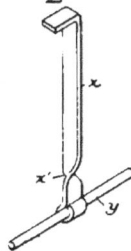

WITNESSES

E   F.

G   H.

INVENTOR

A.   B.

C.   D.

ATTORNEYS

Note :—The above illustrates a drawing made in accordance with the rules. It shows, upon a scale about *one-half* that of the actual drawing, the relative proportions of the sheet, the margin, the blank space required to be left at the top of the sheet below the margin line, the spaces to be left for the signatures, etc. The drawing board upon which this is printed is a sample of bristol board as required and accepted by the Patent Office.

According to a recent decision, the Patent Office will no longer knowingly accept informal drawings or lithographs, even for the purpose of examination. All drawings must be hand made, with India ink, upon white, smooth surfaced drawing board equal in thickness to three-sheet bristol board. The sheets must measure exactly ten inches wide by fifteen inches high. The margin line must be drawn exactly one inch from the edge of the sheet.

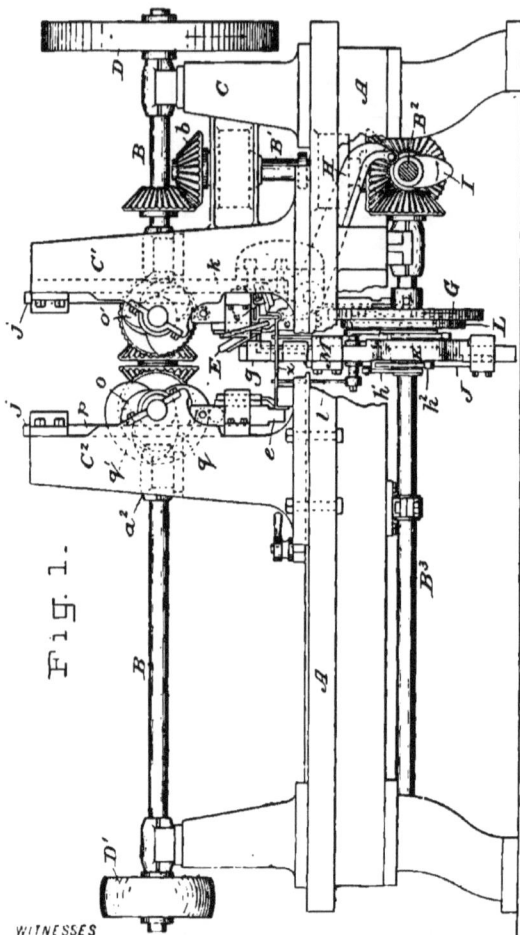

(A clear space of 1¼ inches must be left here for the Heading and Title that is inserted by the Patent Office.)

Fig. 1.

WITNESSES

E   F

G   H

INVENTOR

A.   B.

BY

C.   D

ATTORNEYS

NOTE:—The above illustrates a drawing made in accordance with the rules, where the figure, on account of its size, is placed lengthwise of the sheet. It will be observed that all requirements as to size of sheet, margin, space for heading, and space for signatures, are the same as for other drawings, and that the spaces are to be left at the same relative positions upon the sheet.

See note at the bottom of the preceding page.

space of not less than 1¼ inches (3.2 cm.) must be left blank for the heading, which is inserted by the Patent Office. Care must be taken that no portion of the drawing trespass within this space. Space for the signatures should be reserved at the bottom of the sheet above the marginal line.

LARGE VIEWS.—When views are larger (broader) than the width of the sheet, the sheet should be turned on its side. In this case space for the heading will be reserved at the right, and for the signatures at the left of the sheet, occupying the same position as in the upright views, and being horizontal when the sheet is held in an upright position, that is to say, these spaces for heading and signature always occupy the same positions on the sheet, whichever way the drawing itself may be placed.

POSITION OF VIEWS. All views (and reference letters) on the same sheet must stand in the same direction.

INK, CHARACTER AND COLOR OF LINES.—All drawings must be made with the pen only. Every line and letter must be absolutely black. India ink alone must be used, to secure perfectly black and solid lines. All lines must be clean, sharp, and solid, and they must not be too fine or crowded. This rule applies to all lines, however fine, to shading, and to lines representing cut surfaces in sectional views.

Drawings should be made with the fewest lines possible consistent with clearness. Surface shading when used, should be open. Sectional shading should be made by oblique parallel lines, which may be about one-twentieth of an inch apart. Shading (except upon sectional views) should be used only on convex and concave surfaces, where it should be used sparingly, and even there may be dispensed with if the drawing is otherwise well executed. Imitations of wood or surface graining should not be attempted.

The light is always supposed to come from the upper left hand corner at an angle of forty-five degrees. Heavy lines on the shade sides of objects should be used, except where they tend to thicken the work and obscure the letters of reference.

The plane upon which a sectional view is taken should be indicated upon the general view by a broken or dotted line.

SCALE OF DRAWING. The scale upon which the drawing is made need not be indicated upon the drawing. It should be large enough, in all cases, to show the mechanism without crowding.

LETTERS AND FIGURES OF REFERENCE. The different views should be consecutively numbered. If the same parts of an invention appear in more than one view it must always be represented by the same reference character. The same reference character should never be used to designate different parts, even in different views. Either letters or numerals may be used as reference characters. All letters and figures of reference must be carefully formed. They should measure at least one-eighth of an inch in height, and may be much larger when there is sufficient room. They must be so placed as to clearly indicate to what parts they refer, and at the same time so as never to interfere with the thorough comprehension of the parts themselves. When necessarily grouped around a certain part, they should be placed at a little distance therefrom, where there is available space, and be connected by short broken lines with the parts to which they refer. They must never appear upon shaded surfaces, and when it is difficult to avoid this, a blank space must be left in the shading where the letter occurs, so that it shall appear perfectly distinct and separate from the work.

LITHOGRAPHS. Lithographs will never be accepted under any circumstances, and it is useless to send them. A lithograph drawing if formal in other particulars, may be accepted for the purposes of examination, but in such case a formal drawing will be required, and must be furnished before the application will be allowed.

SIGNATURES. The inventor need not, and preferably should not, sign the drawing, as this can be signed by the attorney under power, but if signed by the inventor, his signature should be placed at the lower right-hand corner of the sheet, and the signatures of two witnesses at the lower left-hand corner, all above and within the marginal line, but in no case should they trespass upon the drawings.

ADVERTISEMENTS NOT PERMITTED.—No advertisement of any nature, or agent's or attorney's stamp, or written address, will be permitted upon the face of the drawing, either within or without the marginal line.

DRAWINGS FOR RE-ISSUE APPLICATIONS.—Drawings for re-issue applications must be made upon the same scale as the original drawings, or upon a larger scale, unless a reduction of scale shall be authorized by the Commissioner.

(E.) MODEL OR SPECIMEN.

A model will only be required or admitted as a part of the application when on examination of the case the Examiner shall find it to be necessary or useful. In such case, the examiner will notify the applicant of such requirement, which will constitute an official action in the case.   When a model is required the examination will be suspended until it shall have been filed.

Under the present practice of the Patent Office models are only required :

(*a.*) When the invention cannot be clearly and fully understood from the specifications and drawings filed.

(*b.*) When it is believed that the alleged invention is inoperative.

Models are now required in all cases where the invention relates to " perpetual motion " or devices for ": increasing power," before any examination will be made as to novelty.

REQUISITES OF MODEL.—The model must clearly show every feature of the invention, but should not include other matter than that covered by the actual invention or improvement, unless it be necessary to the exhibition of the invention in a working model.

The model must be neatly and substantially made of durable material, metal being deemed preferable ; but when the material forms an essential feature of the invention, the model will be constructed of that material.   The model must not be more than one foot in length, width, or height, except in cases in which the Commissioner shall admit working models of complicated machines of larger dimensions.   If made of wood, it must be painted or varnished. Glue must not be used ; but the parts should be so connected as to resist the action of heat or moisture.   When practicable, to prevent loss, the model or specimen should have the name of the inventor permanently fixed thereon.   In cases where models are not made strong and substantial, as here directed, the application will not be examined until a proper model is furnished.

SPECIMEN.—If the invention or discovery is a composition of matter, the Commissioner may call upon the applicant to furnish specimens of the composition, and of its ingredients, sufficient in quantity for the purpose of experiment.   This requirement is, however, seldom made.

THE EXAMINATION AND PROSECUTION OF THE APPLICATION.

The examination of applications is conducted by thirty-two principal (primary) examiners, each in charge of certain classes of inventions, assisted by thirty-four first, thirty-eight second, forty-three third and fifty-three fourth assistant examiners, and numerous clerks and copyists.

Upon the receipt of the application at the Patent Office it is first entered of record in the office of the Chief Clerk.   The Financial Clerk sees that the first government fee of fifteen dollars is paid ; the Application Clerk that all formalities as to signatures and the oath have been properly complied with ; the Chief Draughtsman that the drawing is made in conformity to the rules.   If the application is not complete and correct in these particulars the papers are returned for correction ; if found correct the application receives a filing date and serial number, and is then sent to the examiner in charge of the class of inventions to which it belongs, and a receipt is forwarded to the applicant stating the filing date and the number of the application, and that it " will be taken up for examination in its order."   Inventions are classified in two hundred and three general classes, which are again subdivided into more than four thousand sub-classes.   An application will be reached for examination in from one to six months or more after it has been filed, some examiners being further behind in their work than others.

EXAMINATION AS TO FORM.

The first step in the examination is to determine whether the application is in all respects in proper form.   All the parts of the application are subjected to a rigid scrutiny and all errors or omissions must be cured by amendment.   If the technical terms employed are not correct they must be changed.   If more than one invention is claimed, a division of the application is demanded, in which the inventor is required to limit his claims to a single invention.   He may in such case file separate applications for the matter eliminated, if he wishes to do so.   If the drawing is not sufficiently full to clearly show the invention, additional views will be called for.   If the specification is faulty, or does not fully describe the invention it must be revised and made complete.   If the claims are not properly drawn they must be revised and corrected.

EXAMINATION AS TO NOVELTY.

The examiner then proceeds to examine the case as to its merits, *i. e.*, to determine whether the invention is new and useful.   These examinations are usually very thoroughly conducted.   The drawings of all prior patents in the class to which the invention belongs, and those in other classes, where there is a possibility that there may be any analogy, are carefully compared with those of the pending application.   Not only prior United States patents, but the prior patents of all countries, and also the printed publications in the Patent Office Library are examined.   The result of the examination is communicated to the applicant through his attorney, and in the great majority of cases consists of a rejection, or partial rejection of the claims presented, with the reasons therefor, and such information, and reference to prior patents or publications as will be useful to the applicant in the further prosecution of the application.

A REJECTION IS NOT A FINAL REFUSAL OF A PATENT.

It should be noted here that such a rejection is not a definite and final refusal to grant a patent. The examinaton is made with more particular reference to what *is claimed* than what *is shown* in the application, and while the invention itself may be entirely new and novel, and therefore patentable, the examiner may properly reject the claims presented for the reason that they are so worded that they describe old and well known devices as well as they do the applicant's invention. It frequently happens that an examiner rejects an application upon reference to a patent, the substance of which he considers to be entirely different from the applicant's invention, because the applicant's claims cover matter which is shown in a prior patent or has been described in some printed publication.

RIGHT TO AMEND.

The applicant has 'a right to amend before or after the first rejection or action ; and he may amend as often as the examiner presents new references or reasons for rejection. In so amending, the applicant must clearly point out all the patentable novelty which he thinks his invention presents in view of the state of the art disclosed by the references cited, or the objections made. He must also show how the amendments avoid such references or objections.

The object of such amendments is, of course, to correct errors and omissions in the specification and drawings, and to limit the claims to the precise features of novelty contained in the invention, and this right to amend is one of the most valuable features of the United States patent law and practice. The examiner having rejected the claims of an application upon reference to prior patents or publications, it becomes incumbent upon the applicant to overcome these objections by revising his specifications and claims so as to point out sharply and clearly the features of novelty in his invention, and to avoid claiming that that is old and well known as shown in the references cited. This may be done in most cases by re-writing the claims. Oftentimes the change of one or two words in a claim will be sufficient, and cause the examiner to allow it, when otherwise he would not. In other cases a portion of, or the entire specification and claims must be rewritten, and perhaps the drawings amended. Great skill is required to so word the claims that they shall clearly identify the invention and separate it from all prior ones, and at the same time make the claims as broad as the invention. Such an amendment having been filed, the examiner again takes up the application for consideration and continues his examination. He may, and usually does find and cite new references, or objections, and additional amendments are required to overcome them. In this way from one to a dozen or more letters are written by the examiner, and as many amendments filed before the case is disposed of by an allowance of the patent or a final rejection of the application. A rejection is not final until the examiner has twice rejected the same claim upon the same references or same state of facts.

ALLOWANCE AND ISSUE OF PATENT.

When the examination shows that the applicant is justly entitled to a patent for the invention as claimed by him, the examiner "allows " the patent, and notice of such allowance is mailed to the applicant through his attorney. The inventor can then pay the final government fee of $20, at any time within six months from the date of the allowance. All patents are issued upon the third Tuesday after the first Thursday following the day upon which the final fee is received at the Patent Office. The intervening time is employed in preparing the patent, printing the specification, and photo-lithographing the drawings.

RENEWAL OF FORFEITED APPLICATIONS.

A forfeited application is one upon which a patent has been withheld because of failure to pay the final fee within the prescribed time.

When the patent has been withheld by reason of non-payment of the final fee, any person, whether inventor or assignee, who has an interest in the invention for which such patent was ordered to issue, may file a renewal of the application for the same invention ; but such second application must be made within two years after the allowance of the original application. Upon the hearing of such new application abandonment will be considered as a question of fact.

In such renewal the oath, petition, specification, drawing, and model of the original application may be used for the second application ; but a new fee will be required. The second application will not be regarded for all purposes as a continuation of the original one, but must bear date from the time of renewal, and be subject to examination like an original application.

APPEALS.

INTERLOCUTORY APPEALS AS TO QUESTIONS OF FORM.

Any proper question, which has been twice acted upon by the examiner, and which does not involve the merits of the invention claimed, or the rejection of a claim, may be appealed directly to the Commissioner of Patents. No government fee is required for such a petition.

Such an appeal may also be taken if the primary examiner refuses to admit an amendment.

APPEALS TO THE EXAMINERS-IN-CHIEF.

Every applicant for a patent, any of the claims of whose application have been twice rejected for the same reasons, upon grounds involving the merits of the invention, such as lack of invention, novelty, or utility, or on the ground of abandonment, public use or sale, inoperativeness of invention, aggregation of elements, incomplete combination of elements, or when amended, for want of identity with the invention originally disclosed, or because the amendment involves a departure from the invention originally presented ; and every applicant for the re-issue of a patent, whose claims have been twice rejected for any of the reasons above enumerated, or on the ground that the original patent is not "inoperative or invalid," or if so inoperative or invalid that the errors which rendered it so did not arise from "inadvertence, accident, or mistake," may appeal from the decision of the primary examiner to the examiners-in-chief. The appeal must set forth in writing the points of the decision upon which it is taken, and must be signed by the applicant or his duly authorized attorney or agent.

There must have been two rejections of the claims as originally filed, or, if amended in matter of substance, of the amended claims, and all the claims must have been passed upon, and all preliminary and intermediate questions relating to matters not affecting the merits of the invention settled, before the case can be appealed to the examiners-in-chief.

Upon the filing of the appeal the same is submitted to the primary examiner, who, if he finds it to be regular in form, furnishes the examiners-in-chief with a written statement of the grounds of his decision on all the points involved in the appeal, with copies of the rejected claims, and with the references applicable thereto. If the primary examiner decides that the appeal is not regular in form, a petition from such decision may be taken directly to the Commissioner.

The appellant before the day of hearing is required to file a brief of the authorities and arguments on which he will rely to maintain his appeal.

If the appellant desires to be heard orally before the examiners-in-chief, he must so indicate when he files his appeal; a day of hearing will then be fixed, and due notice of the same given him.

In contested cases the appellant has the right to make the opening and closing arguments, unless it shall be otherwise ordered by the tribunal having jurisdiction of the case.

The examiners-in-chief then hear the appeal, and in their decision affirm or reverse the decision of the primary examiner on the points on which appeal has been taken.

Should they discover any apparent grounds not involved in the appeal for granting or refusing letters patent in the form claimed, or in any other form, they will annex to their decision a statement to that effect, with such recommendation as they shall deem proper.

From an adverse judgment of the primary examiner on points embraced in the recommendation annexed to the decision, appeal may be taken on questions involving the merits to the board of examiners-in-chief and on other questions to the Commissioner, as in other cases

FROM THE EXAMINERS-IN-CHIEF TO THE COMMISSIONER OF PATENTS.

From an adverse decision of the board of examiners-in-chief, appeal may be taken to the Commissioner in person, who will hear and render decision upon the question in issue.

FROM THE COMMISSIONER OF PATENTS TO THE SUPREME COURT OF THE DISTRICT OF COLUMBIA.

From an adverse decision of the Commissioner upon the claims of an application an appeal may be taken to the Supreme Court of the District of Columbia sitting *in banc*. On taking such appeal, the applicant is required, under the rules of the court, to pay to the clerk of the court a docket-fee, and he is also required by law to lay before the court certified copies of all the original papers and evidence in the case. The petition should be filed and the fee paid at least ten days before the commencement of the term of court at which the appeal is to be heard.

Hearings of the appeal are subject to the rules of the court as provided for other causes therein.

APPEALS IN INTERFERENCE CASES.

In interference cases parties have the same remedy by appeal to the examiners-in-chief and to the Commissioner as in *ex parte* cases; but no appeal lies in such cases from the decision of the Commissioner. Defeated contestants in interferences may, however, have remedy by bill in equity.

Appeals in interference cases must be accompanied by brief statements of the reasons therefor; and parties will be required to file briefs of their arguments before the day of hearing.

Printed briefs are required in all cases.

RE-ISSUES.

Whenever an original patent is inoperative or invalid by reason of a defective or insufficient specification, or by reason of the patentee claiming as his invention or discovery more than he had a right to claim as new, provided the error has arisen through inadvertence, accident, or mistake, and without any fraudulent or deceptive intention, the original patent may be surrendered and a new or re-issued patent will be issued in place thereof. The sole purpose of a re-issue is to correct faults of statement in the description and claim of the original patent. A re-issue cannot claim either another invention or a broader invention than the one attempted to be described and claimed in the original patent; nor can it claim matter expressly or impliedly excluded from the invention by the original patent; nor, can a claim rejected by the Patent Office, and the rejection acquiesced in, be re-instated by a re-issue. A mistake of a Solicitor in procuring a patent with claims narrower than he was instructed to make cannot be cured by re-issue after years of delay. A claim can be enlarged in a re-issue only when an actual mistake has occurred, not from a mere error of judgment, but a real *bona fide* mistake, inadvertently committed, such as a court of chancery in cases within its ordinary jurisdiction would correct, and the application for the re-issue must be filed within a reasonable time. Under the present decisions of the courts the application for a re-issue, if the only object is to enlarge the claims, must not be delayed long after the issue of the original patent. In Ives *v.* Sargent, 38 O. G. 781, it was held that an excuse for a delay longer than two years must be clearly shown; in Arnheim *v.* Finster, 34 O. G. 700, that where the error, if any, is apparent and the articles claimed in the re-issue have gone into the market, twenty-two months is too long a delay; and in Coon *v.* Wilson, 30 O. G. 889, that a delay of three months in applying for a re-issue is unreasonable when the defect is clear and other claimants intervene, if the only object is to enlarge the original claims. A void patent cannot be re-issued to cure defects.

WHO MAY OBTAIN A RE-ISSUE.

A re-issue will be granted to the original patentee, his legal representatives, or the assignees of the entire interest, but the application must be made, and the specification sworn to by the inventor, if he be living.

THE APPLICATION FOR A RE-ISSUE.

A complete application for the re-issue of a patent consists of the following parts :
    (1.) A Petition (with Power of Attorney, if an Attorney is appointed).
    (2.) Specification with Claims.
    (3.) Drawing, if the invention can be illustrated.
    (4.) Oath.
    (5.) An abstract of title.
    (6.) The original patent.

The petition for a re-issue must be accompanied by a certified copy of the abstract of title, giving the names of all assignees owning any undivided interest in the patent. In case the application be made by the inventor, it must be accompanied by the written assent of such assignees. All the owners of the patent must concur in the surrender either by consent or ratification.

NEW MATTER NOT ALLOWED.

New matter is not allowed to be introduced into the re-issue specification, nor in case of a machine can the model or drawings be amended except each by the other; but when there is neither model nor drawing, amendments may be made upon proof satisfactory to the Commissioner that such new matter or amendment was a part of the original invention and was omitted from the specification by inadvertence, accident, or mistake.

THE OATH REQUIRED.

Applicants for re-issue, must file with their petitions a statement on oath as follows:

(1.) That applicant verily believes the original patent to be inoperative or invalid, and the reason why.

(2.) When it is claimed that such patent is so inoperative or invalid " by reason of a defective or insufficient specification," particularly specifying such defects or insufficiencies.

(3.) When it is claimed that such patent is inoperative or invalid " by reason of the patentee claiming as his own invention or discovery more than he had a right to claim as new," distinctly specifying the part or parts so alleged to have been improperly claimed as new.

(4.) Particularly specifying the errors which it is claimed constitute the inadvertence, accident, or mistake relied upon, and how they arose or occurred.

(5.) That said errors arose "without any fraudulent or deceptive intention " on the part of the applicant.

EXAMINATION.

An original claim, if reproduced in the re-issue specification, is subject to re-examination, and the entire application will be revised and restricted in the same manner as original applications.

SURRENDER OF ORIGINAL PATENT.

The application for a re-issue must be accompanied by a surrender of the original patent, or, if that be lost, by an affidavit to that effect, and a certified copy of the patent ; but if a re-issue be refused, the original patent will, upon request, be returned to the applicant.

INTERFERENCES.

An interference is a proceeding instituted in the Patent Office for the purpose of determining the priority of the inventive act between two or more parties claiming substantially the same patentable invention. The intent of the law is that a patent shall be granted to the first and original inventor. Where there are rival claimants for the same invention it becomes the duty of the Patent Office to ascertain which of the claimants is the true and first inventor. To determine this fact a judicial proceeding is instituted in which each of the claimants is required to prove the date upon which he conceived the invention, each of the parties having the right to be heard by evidence and argument in defense of his own claims and in opposition to the claims of his opponents. When all the testimony has been taken the examiner of interferences passes upon the evidence and declares which of the claimants appears to be the true and first inventor and is entitled to a patent. This judicial proceeding is called an Interference.

WHEN DECLARED.

Interferences will be declared in the following cases, when all the parties claim substantially the same patentable invention :

(1.) Between two or more original applications containing conflicting claims.

(2.) Between an original application and an unexpired patent containing conflicting claims, when the applicant, having been rejected on the patent, shall file an affidavit that he made the invention before the patentee's application was filed.

(3.) Between an original application and an application for the re-issue of a patent granted during the pendency of such original application.

(4.) Between an original application and a re-issue application, when the original applicant shall file an affidavit showing that he made the invention before the patentee's original application was filed.

(5.) Between two or more applications for the re-issue of patents granted on applications pending at the same time.

(6.) Between two or more applications for the re-issue of patents granted on applications not pending at the same time, when the applicant for re-issue of the later patent shall file an affidavit showing that he made the invention before the application was filed on which the earlier patent was granted.

(7.) Between a re-issue application and an unexpired patent, if the original applications were pending at the same time, and the re-issue applicant shall file an affidavit showing that he made the invention before the original application of the other patentee was filed.

(8.) Between an application for re-issue of a later unexpired patent and an earlier unexpired patent granted before the original application of the later patent was filed, if the re-issue applicant shall file an affidavit showing that he made the invention before the original application of the earlier patent was filed.

In this connection it should be noted that an interference between two or more existing patents cannot be adjudicated in the Patent Office ; that an interference cannot be declared against an expired patent ; and that no interference can be declared with forfeited or abandoned applications. Under former rules of the Patent Office, an interference was declared where applications might be amended so as to include conflicting claims, although the conflicting matter was not so claimed at the time the interference was instituted. At the present time the rules forbid the declaration of an interference until the conflict appears specifically in the claims.

PROCEDURE IN INTERFERENCE CASES.

When a primary examiner finds that the claims of any applicant for patent are the same or substantially the same as those of another applicant (or patentee under the conditions set forth in sub-sections (2), (7) and (8) above) it becomes his duty to forward the papers in the case to the examiner of interferences, who reviews them and if found correct will declare the interference and send notices of the same to the parties interested. No interference will be declared until all preliminary questions have been settled by the primary examiner, and the invention decided to be patentable.

The first step in an interference is the filing of a preliminary statement, under oath, by each of the parties thereto, on or before a date to be fixed by the Patent Office, in which foreign inventors are required to set forth the following facts:—

(1.) That applicant made the invention set forth in the declaration of interference.

(2.) Whether or not the invention was ever patented : if so, when and where, giving the date and number of each patent.

(3) Whether or not the invention was ever described in a printed publication ; if so, when and where, giving the title, place, and date of such publication.

(4.) When the invention or the knowledge of it was introduced into this country ; giving the circumstances, with the dates connected therewith, which are relied upon to establish the fact.

The preliminary statements should be carefully prepared, as the parties will be strictly held in their proofs to the dates set up therein.

If a party refuse or neglect to file a statement, testimony will not be received subsequently from him to prove that he made the invention at a date prior to his application for patent. If on examination a statement is found to be defective, a time is assigned within which the defect may be cured.

When the time for filing the statements has elapsed, the statements are examined and compared with the the original applications. If the date of the filing of the earliest application is not anticipated by the dates fixed by the other parties for their own conception of the invention, priority is awarded to the earliest applicant. If the date of a later applicant fails to carry the date of his inventive act behind the date when the earlier applications were filed, judgment is entered against him. Only in cases where the date of invention claimed in a preliminary statement is earlier than the date of the filing of an earlier application does the interference proceed further, since in these cases alone is the *prima facie* presumption of priority arising from the dates of filing the respective applications rebutted, and additional evidence necessary to determine which of the claimants was actually the first inventor.

TAKING TESTIMONY.

In all cases where such further evidence is necessary, certain times are fixed by the examiner within which the testimony of the several parties must be taken. The same rules as to evidence apply in interference cases as in the courts of the United States. Notice must be given by parties of the time when, and place where, the testimony will be taken, and full opportunity must be afforded for the opponent to cross-examine the witnesses either in person or by attorney. The time for taking testimony may be extended in favor of either party upon a motion disclosing under oath the reasons for his inability to obtain his evidence within the time prescribed, the names of the witnesses whose testimony he desires, the facts which he expects to prove by them, and the efforts he has made to secure their earlier attendance. All evidence must be given under oath, and must be written out by, or in the presence of the officer before whom the deposition is taken, who must certify thereto and affix his seal of office.

FORWARDING TESTIMONY.

The deposition must be carefully read over by the witness, or by the officer to him, and is then subscribed by the witness in the presence of the officer. The officer must annex to the deposition his certificate, showing

(1.) The due administration of the oath by the officer to the witness before the commencement of his testimony.

(2.) The name of the person by whom the testimony was written out, and the fact that, if not written by the officer, it was written in his presence.

(3.) The presence or absence of the adverse party.

(4.) The place, day, and hour of commencing and taking the deposition ; and

(5.) The fact that the officer was not connected by blood or marriage with either of the parties, nor interested, directly or indirectly, in the matter in controversy.

The officer must sign the certificate and affix thereto his seal of office. He must then, without delay, securely seal up all the evidence, notices, and paper exhibits, inscribe upon the envelope a certificate, giving the title of the case, the name of each witness, and the date of sealing, address the package, and forward the same to the Commissioner of Patents.

TESTIMONY REQUIRED TO BE PRINTED.

The testimony is required to be printed and six or more printed copies must be furnished for the use of the Patent Office and the opposing parties. When the evidence is all in, a day is fixed by the examiner of interferences for the hearing, when oral arguments may be made by the parties or their attorneys. The examiner then takes the case under consideration and decides as to the priority of invention.

AS TO FOREIGN PATENTEES.

While the law makes no distinction between citizens and foreigners as applicants in the Patent Office it makes a wide distinction between an invention made in the United States and an invention made in a foreign country, whether by a citizen or alien. Under our law no notice is, or can be taken of any inventive act performed abroad until its result is published either in a patent or a printed book. At whatever date therefore, an unpatented or unpublished foreign invention may have been conceived in fact, its conception in the United States takes place only when knowledge of the invention is brought to the United States. In interference proceedings therefore, a foreign patentee cannot prove an earlier date for his invention than the date of his foreign patent or other publication of the invention, should this be earlier than the date upon which knowledge of the invention was brought into the United States (Rumpff v. Köhler, 23 O. G. 1831), and a foreign inventor who has not patented his invention abroad, is limited in his proof of the date of his invention to the date upon which knowledge of the invention was brought to the United States (Thomas v. Reese, 17 O. G., 195).

DISCLAIMERS.

Whenever a patentee has claimed more than he had a right to claim as new and as of his invention, he may abandon the excess by filing a disclaimer of such parts of the thing patented as were not invented by him, and the patent will then be valid for all that part which is truly and justly his own. A disclaimer is thus an inexpensive and expeditious manner of curing a defect that would otherwise be fatal to the patent.

WHO MAY FILE.

A disclaimer may be made by the patentee so long as he is the owner of the patent, or by his heirs or assigns whether of the whole or any sectional interest.

The original patentee cannot disclaim after he has parted with his entire title to the patent, nor can an owner of an undivided interest disclaim without the consent and co-operation of the other owners of the same interest. But an owner either of the entire interest, or of the entire interest within a specified territory, may file a disclaimer, which will have effect to the extent of the interest possessed by the disclaimant, and will thereafter limit and define his rights.

REQUISITES OF DISCLAIMER.

A disclaimer must be in writing, must be signed by the disclaimant, and attested by one or more witnesses, and recorded in the Patent Office. It must set forth the exact interest of the disclaimant, and must particularly state the excess disclaimed, and aver that it was included in the patent through inadvertence, accident, or mistake.

CAVEATS.

WHO MAY FILE.

A caveat can only be filed by a citizen of the United States, or by an alien who has resided in the United States one year preceding the filing of his caveat, and has made oath of his intention to become a citizen.

OBJECT AND FORCE OF CAVEATS.

A caveat is a written notice to the Patent Office that the caveator claims to be the inventor of the invention described, and its effect is to prevent the grant of a patent for the same invention to another party, without notice to the caveator, during the life of the caveat. If, during the life of the caveat another person files such an application, and the invention is found to be patentable, the application will be suspended, and notice thereof sent to the caveator, who may then, within three months thereafter, file his application for patent. He will then be entitled to an interference with the previous application for the purpose of proving priority of invention, and obtaining the patent if he be adjudged the prior inventor.

A caveat confers no rights and affords no protection save the above. It may, however, be used as evidence in contests.

TERM.

A caveat is operative for one year from the filing thereof, and may be renewed from year to year upon payment of the renewal fees.

REQUISITES.

A Caveat must comprise :

(*a.*) A petition (with power of attorney if an attorney is appointed).
(*b.*) A specification.
(*c.*) An oath, and
(*d.*) When the nature of the invention admits of it, a drawing.

The caveat, like an application for patent, must be limited to a single invention. The same particularity of description is not required in a caveat as in an application for patent ; but the caveat must set forth the object of the invention and the distinguishing characteristics thereof, and it should be sufficiently precise to enable the office to judge whether there is a probable interference when a subsequent application is filed for a similar invention.

If, upon examination, a caveat be found defective in this respect, amendment will be required.

The oath must set forth :

(*a.*) That the caveator is a citizen of the United States, or, if he be an alien, that he has resided for one year next preceding within the United States, and has made oath of his intention to become a citizen thereof, and

(*b.*) That he believes himself to be the original and first inventor of the invention set forth in his caveat.

The drawings should be well executed on tracing muslin or paper that may be folded.

ASSIGNMENTS.

An invention may be assigned and the assignment recorded, at any time, either before or after the application for patent is made, or the patent granted. The assignment may be for either the right to make, use, or sell, or for the right to do all these acts, and may be for the whole or any specified part of the United States. Undivided interests may also be assigned.

Interests in patents may be vested in assignees, in grantees of exclusive sectional rights, in mortgagees, and in licencees, and any instrument amounting to an assignment, grant, mortgage, lien, incumbrance, or licence, or which affects the title of the patent, or invention to which it relates, may be entered of record. Assignments which are made conditional upon the performance of certain stipulations, such as the payment of money, if recorded, are regarded as absolute assignments, until canceled with the written consent of both parties, or by the decree of a competent court. A single assignment may include more than one patent, although to avoid confusion on the records, a separate assignment for each patent is desirable.

MUST BE RECORDED.

An assignment, grant, or conveyance of a patent will be void as against any subsequent purchaser or mortgagee for a valuable consideration without notice unless recorded in the Patent Office within three months from the date thereof.

FORM.

No particular form of assignment is prescribed. It is, however, desirable to use the forms recommended by the Patent Office (See Forms) so far as practicable.

MUST IDENTIFY THE INVENTION OR PATENT.

The assignment should identify the patent by date and number ; or, if the invention be unpatented, by the name of the inventor, the serial number, and the date of the filing of the application ; or, in case of assignments executed co-incidently with the application, by the name of the inventor, the title of invention, and the date of the execution of the documents.

PATENTED ARTICLES SHOULD BE MARKED.

It is the duty of all patentees, and their assigns and legal representatives, and of all persons making or vending any patented article for or under them, to give sufficient notice to the public that the same is patented ; either by affixing thereon the word "patented," together with the day and year the patent was granted ; or when, from the character of the article, this can not be done, by fixing to it, or to the package wherein one or more of them is inclosed, a label containing the like notice ; and in any suit for infringement, by the party failing so to mark, no damages can be recovered by the plaintiff, except on proof that the defendant was duly notified of the infringement, and continued, after such notice, to make, use, or vend the article so patented.

Persons falsely marking or labeling articles as patented, are liable to a penalty of one hundred dollars for each offense, one-half of said penalty to be paid to the person who shall sue for same.

DESIGN PATENTS.

TO WHOM GRANTED, TERM AND REQUIREMENTS.

Patents for useful and ornamental designs are granted to the true and first inventor, for the term of three and one-half, seven, or fourteen years, as the applicant may, in his application elect.   Short term patents cannot be prolonged.

The requirements and proceedings for patents for designs are substantially the same as for applications for other patents.   The specification must distinctly point out the characteristic features of the design, and carefully distinguish between what is old and what is believed to be new.   The claims also, when the design admits of it, should be as distinct and specific as in the case of other applications.

DOCUMENTS REQUIRED.

The documents required are :

(a.) Petition, (with power of attorney if an attorney is appointed.)
(b.) Specification.
(c.) Oath.
(d.) A drawing or photographs.

When the design cannot be sufficiently represented by drawings or photographs, a model will be required.

DRAWING OR PHOTOGRAPHS.

The design must, if possible, be represented by a drawing made in conformity with the rules prescribed for drawings for mechanical patents.

In case the nature of the design is such that it cannot be properly represented by such a drawing, upon the representation of the Examiner a photograph may be employed.

Whenever a photograph is furnished it must be mounted upon a sheet of Bristol board of the kind and dimensions prescribed for drawings of other patents, and the applicant must furnish not less than twenty-five extra unmounted copies of such photographs of a size not exceeding seven and a half inches by eleven.   (19x28 cm.)

EXAMINATION.

The examination as to form of documents and novelty, and the prosecution and amendment of applications is precisely the same as in the case of applications for mechanical patents.

PATENTED ARTICLES SHOULD BE MARKED.

The requirements as to the marking of articles protected by design patents are the same as in the case of mechanical patents.

ASSIGNMENTS.

The requirements and practice is the same as for mechanical patents.

TRADE MARKS.

WHO MAY REGISTER.

A person, firm, or corporation, the owner of any trade mark used in commerce between the United States and any foreign nation or with the Indian tribes, provided such owner shall be domiciled in the United States, or located in any foreign country or tribes, which by treaty, convention, or law, affords similar protection to citizens of the United States. The United States has concluded trade mark treaties with the following Governments, and upon the following dates :—Austria-Hungary, June 1, 1872 ; Belgium, July 30, 1869 and July 9, 1884 ; Brazil, Sept. 24, 1878 ; France, April 16, 1869 ; German Empire, June 1, 1872 ; Great Britain (including British Colonies so far as they grant reciprocal protection to citizens of the United States), July 17, 1878 ; Italy, March 19, 1884 ; Netherlands, Feb. 16, 1883 ; Russia, June 27, 1868 ; Servia, Dec. 27, 1882 ; Spain, April 19, 1883 ; Switzerland, May 16, 1883.

The United States is also a member of the International Convention, and residents of countries belonging to this Union may obtain registration.

TERM OF PROTECTION.

The term of registration is thirty years, renewable for an additional term of thirty years, but in case of trade marks registered in other countries for a shorter period, the protection in this country ceases at the time such trade mark ceases to be exclusive property elsewhere.

WHAT MAY BE REGISTERED.

The statute does not define the word " trade mark", or say of what it shall consist. The term is used as though its signification were already well known in the law. Resort must therefore be had to the law outside of the statute, to ascertain what is or what may become a lawful trade mark.

In general it may be said that any arbitrary mark or device, that has been so long used in connection with an article of manufacture that it has become well known to the trade as designating a particular person's goods, constitutes a lawful trade mark; but no trade mark will be registered unless the same appear to be lawfully used as such by the applicant in foreign commerce or commerce with Indian tribes, or is within the provision of a treaty, convention, or declaration with a foreign power; nor which is merely the name of the applicant; nor which is identical with a registered or known trade mark owned by another and appropriate to the same class of merchandise, or which so nearly resembles some other person's lawful trade mark as to be likely to cause confusion or mistake in the mind of the public, or to deceive purchasers.

The autograph or name of the owner, provided it be written, printed, branded, or stamped in a mode peculiar to itself; a seal, picture, cipher, monogram, or a combination of any of these; a mere word, a combination of words, a letter, or combination of letters not recognized as a word, or any other sign or symbol that can serve to distinguish the products of one man from another may be a valid trade mark provided it is an arbitrary device and not descriptive, and not a word in common use.

It is no bar to the registry of a trade mark that it has already been used as such on articles of a different character, and it is only necessary that the trade mark be so far original as that when known in the market the goods of one merchant or manufacturer may be distinguished from those of another.

UNREGISTERABLE.

A word that is descriptive cannot be registered, nor can a simple outline figure surrounding a word or words purely descriptive of the article or the quality be registered as a trade mark.

It has been decided by the Courts that a trade mark which consists merely of the name of a person not arranged in a mode peculiar to itself, cannot be registered, although it is accompanied by a mark sufficient to distinguish it from the same name when used by others; that a geographical name although it is joined with something else is not a proper trade mark for registration; and that a trade mark that is deceptive or misleading either as to the place of manufacture, the name or address of the manufacturer or vendor, the class of product or quality, or in any other way, is not a valid trade mark.

USE OF MARK.

A trade mark may be written, printed, stamped, painted, stencilled, branded, or otherwise, and either upon the article itself, or on its case, covering, envelope, or wrapper. The trade mark may also be used in advertisements or upon the stationery of the owner.

THE APPLICATION FOR REGISTRATION.

A complete application for registration consists of the following parts :
- (*a*) Letter of advice, (with power of attorney, if an attorney is appointed.)
- (*b*) A statement or specification of the trade mark.
- (*c*) A declaration or oath.
- (*d*) A drawing of the trade mark.

(*a*) THE LETTER OF ADVICE WITH POWER OF ATTORNEY. The letter of advice should :
- (1) Be addressed to the Commissioner of Patents.
- (2) Should contain a reference to the fac-simile of the trade mark filed therewith, and
- (3) A request that the same be registered in the United States Patent Office in accordance with the law in such cases made and provided.

The power of attorney may be and preferably is joined to the letter of advice, and should be in the same general form and language as in the case of patents.

(*b*) THE STATEMENT OR SPECIFICATION. The statement or specification should contain :
- (1) A preamble stating the name and address of the applicant, and in the case of an individual applicant his citizenship and residence.
- (2) An explicit statement of the essential features of the trade mark claimed.
- (3) A full and clear description of the trade mark and everything relating thereto.
- (4) The date since which the trade mark has been continuously used by applicant.
- (5) A statement of the class of merchandise to which the trade mark is appropriated.
- (6) A statement of the particular description of goods on which it is used.
- (7) A statement of the mode of applying the trade mark.

(*c* THE DECLARATION OR OATH must contain the following allegations :
- (1) That the applicant is the applicant named in the foregoing statement, and that he verily believes the foregoing statement is true.
- (2) That he has at this time a right to the use of the trade mark therein described, and that no other person, firm or corporation has the right to such use, either in the identical form or in any such near resemblance thereto as might be calculated to deceive.
- (3) That it is used by him in commerce between the United States and foreign nations or Indian tribes, *naming one or more of such foreign nations or Indian tribes*, between which and the United States it is so used, and
- (4) That the description and fac-similes presented for record truly represent the trade mark sought to be registered.

(*d*) THE DRAWING. The trade mark must be represented by a drawing which must conform in all respects to the rules prescribed for drawings of mechanical patents. If for any reason the drawing filed does not constitute a satisfactory fac-simile of the trade mark, two copies of the trade mark, as actually used, must be filed in addition to the drawing required. The rules of practice have recently been changed in this particular, and a drawing must now be supplied with every application.

EXECUTION OF DOCUMENTS.

All the documents except the drawing or fac-similes must be signed by the applicant. The signature of the applicant upon the statement must be attested by the signatures of two witnesses. The drawing may, and preferably should be signed by the ,attorney. If signed by the applicant, his signature must appear in the lower right hand corner above the marginal line, and his signature must be attested by the signatures of two witnesses who must sign in the lower left hand corner above the marginal line.

The declaration or oath must be sworn to and signed before a Notary Public or a Consular officer of the United States, who must in all cases affix his official seal.

IN THE CASE OF A FIRM. The letter of advice and the statement or specification should be signed in the firm name, while the declaration should be made by and sworn to by some member of the firm on behalf of such firm.

IN THE CASE OF A CORPORATION. The letter of advice and the statement or specification should be signed in the name of the corporation, together with the signature and title of the officer of the corporation signing same, while the declaration should be made by and sworn to by such official on behalf of the corporation. If the corporation have a seal it should be affixed to authenticate the signature of the officer.

THE EXAMINATION AND AMENDMENTS.

When the application is filed in the Patent Office an examination is made both as to the form of the documents and the novelty of the trade mark. The procedure is substantially the same as in case of applications for patents. If defects exist in any of the documents, except the declaration, they may be cured by amendment. The declaration cannot be amended. If that filed with the application is faulty or defective, a substitute declaration must be filed.

NO REQUIREMENTS AS TO MARKING.

The law contains no provision requiring the owner of a trade mark to warn the public of its registration, it is, however, usual for owners of trade marks to notify the public thereof by printing or otherwise displaying in connection with their trade mark the word "Trade Mark" or the words "Trade Mark Registered."

ASSIGNMENTS.

The right to the use of any registered trade mark is assignable by an instrument in writing, and such assignment of a trade mark must be recorded in the Patent Office within sixty days after its execution, in default of which it may be void as against any subsequent purchaser or mortgagee for a valuable consideration without notice. No particular form of assignment is prescribed, but the trade mark must be identified by the certificate number.

LABELS AND PRINTS.

DEFINED.

The words "prints" and "labels" are construed as synonymous, and are defined as any device, picture, word or words, figure or figures, that do not amount to a trade mark, impressed or stamped directly upon the articles of manufacture, or upon a slip or piece of paper, or other material, to be attached in any manner to manufactured articles, or to bottles, boxes, and packages containing them, to indicate the contents of the package, the name of the manufacturer or the place of manufacture, the quality of goods, directions for use, etc.

Until recently, all forms of prints and labels, even when consisting solely of the name of the manufacturer or the place of manufacture, the quality or quantity of goods, or directions for use, have been registered by the Patent Office ; but the Supreme Court has recently decided, (Higgins et al v. Keuffel et al, 55 O. G. 1139,) that to be entitled to copyright the print or label must have by itself some value as a composition or writing, at least to the extent of serving some purpose other than as a mere advertisement or designation of the subject to which it is attached.

The clause of the Constitution under which Congress is authorized to legislate for the protection of authors and inventors is contained in the eighth section of article one, which declares that—

The Congress shall have power to promote the progress of science and useful arts, by securing for limited times to authors and inventors the exclusive right to their respective writings and discoveries.

The copyright act, and the act of June 18, 1874, under which labels are registered, are based upon this provision. The Supreme Court has therefore held in effect, that this provision has reference only to such writings and discoveries as are the result of intellectual labor, and that labels which simply designate or describe the articles to which they are attached, and which have no value separated from the articles, and no possible influence upon science or the useful arts, are not proper subjects for registration.

Thus a label upon a box of fruit giving its name as "grapes" even with the addition of adjectives characterizing their quality as "black" or "sweet" would not be registerable. Should, however, the label contain an essay upon the culture of grapes, or any other matter relating to science or the useful arts, clearly the product and result of intellectual labor, the label would be entitled to copyright protection.

WHO MAY OBTAIN PROTECTION.

The benefits of the act seem to have been originally confined to citizens or residents of the United States, but have been extended by existing treaties to British, German, Italian, and Belgian subjects.

UNREGISTERABLE.

No print or label can be registered unless it properly belongs to an article of commerce, and be as above defined ; nor can the same be registered when it amounts to a lawful trade mark, or when its use in connection with the article to which it is applied is arbitrary or fanciful.

APPLICATION TO BE FILED BEFORE PUBLICATION.

In order to secure copyright protection for a label or print, it is necessary that the application for its registration be filed in the Patent Office on or before the date of the first publication of such label or print in this or any foreign country. A label or print that has been published cannot be copyrighted upon an application filed subsequent to the date of such publication.

DOCUMENTS REQUIRED.

A complete application for the registration of a label or print consists of the following parts :
(*a.*) An application addressed to the Commissioner of Patents, containing a reference to the label or print presented for registration ; claiming its ownership ; stating its title ; containing a description thereof ; and a request that the same be registered in the Patent Office.
(*b.*) At least five copies of the label or print.
The application must be signed by the applicant. In case of a firm, the usual signature of the firm will be sufficient. If the applicant is a corporation, it should be signed in the name of such corporation by one of the principal officers thereof, who must add his own signature and title of office. His signature should be attested by the corporate seal of the company.

NOTICE OF COPYRIGHT REQUIRED.

The law requires that when copyright of a label or print has been obtained that due notice of such copyright shall be given to the public. All copyrighted labels or prints should therefore contain the following notification : "Copyrighted 1892, by A. B.," or as the case may be, stating the year the copyright was entered, and the name of the party by whom it was taken out.

ASSIGNMENTS.

It is held that a registered label is, like a copyright, assignable by an instrument in writing. No particular form of assignment is prescribed, but the assignment should be presented for record within sixty days of its execution, otherwise it is liable to be held void as against any subsequent purchaser or mortgagee for a valuable consideration without notice.

COPYRIGHTS.

WHO MAY OBTAIN.

The benefits of the copyright act were originally intended to apply to citizens of, or residents in the United States only, but by act of March 3, 1891, the law has been so amended that it applies to citizens or subjects of a foreign state or nation, when such foreign state or nation permits to citizens of the United States the benefit of copyright on substantially the same basis as its own citizens ; or when such foreign state or nation is a party to an international agreement which provides for reciprocity in the grant of copyright, by the terms of which agreement the United States may at its pleasure become a party to such agreement. The existence of either of the above conditions is to be determined by the President of the United States, by proclamation made from time to time as the purposes of the act may require. At the present time the President has, by proclamation dated July 1, 1891, extended the benefits of the copyright act to citizens of France and Switzerland, and to subjects of Belgium and Great Britain, including the British Colonies.

The applicant for copyright protection may be the author, inventor, designer or proprietor of any kind of useful work such as enumerated below, or the executors, administrators or assigns of such person.

WHAT MAY BE COPYRIGHTED.

Any book, map, chart, dramatic or musical composition, engraving, cut, print, or photograph or negative thereof, a painting, drawing, chromo, statuary, and models or designs intended to be perfected as works of the fine arts. The word "print" includes lithographs. The word "book" does not carry with it the requirement that it shall be printed. A book may exist without printing, and such book, when made or composed, is entitled to copyright. A "book" need not be a book in the common and ordinary acceptation of the word, viz.: a volume made up of several sheets bound together, it may be printed only on one sheet. In the case of books published in more than one volume, or of periodicals published in numbers, or of engravings, photographs, or other articles published with variations, a copyright is to be entered for each volume or part of a book, or number of a periodical, or variety as to style, title, or inscription of any other article. A copyright may be secured for a projected work as well as a completed one. The time within which any work entered for copyright may be issued from the press is not limited by any law or regulation, but the courts have held that it should take place within a reasonable time.

EXTENT AND TERM OF PROTECTION.

Copyrights are granted for the term of twenty-eight years from the time of recording the title thereof. Within six months before the expiration of that time, the author, inventor, or designer, if he be still living, or his widow or children, if he be dead, may secure a renewal of the copyright for a further term of fourteen years, making forty-two years in all, by recording the title of the work a second time, and complying with all other regulations in regard to original copyrights, and by causing a copy of the record thereof to be published in one or more newspapers printed in the United States, for the space of four weeks. Such advertisement of renewal is to be made within two months of the date of the renewal certificate.

Upon complying with the provisions of the law, authors, and their executors, administrators and assigns, have the sole liberty of printing, reprinting, publishing, completing, copying, executing, finishing, and vending the work so copyrighted ; and, in the case of a dramatic composition, of publicly performing or representing it, or causing it to be performed or represented by others ; also the exclusive right to dramatize or translate such work within the United States and all its territories.

PREREQUISITES TO COPYRIGHT PROTECTION.

No person will be entitled to a copyright unless he shall, on or before the date of publication, in this or any foreign country, deliver at the office of the Librarian of Congress in Washington, or deposit in the mail within the United States, addressed to the Librarian of Congress, a printed copy of the title of the book, map, chart, dramatic or musical composition, engraving, cut, print, photograph, or chromo, or a description of the painting, drawing, statue, statuary, or a model or design for a work of the fine arts, for which he desires a copyright ; nor unless he shall also, not later than the day of the publication thereof, in this or any foreign country, deliver at the office of the Librarian of Congress, at Washington, District of Columbia, or deposit in the mail within the United States, addressed to the Librarian of Congress, at Washington, District of Columbia, two copies of such copyright book, map, chart, dramatic or musical composition, engraving, chromo, cut, print, or photograph; or in case of a painting, drawing, statue, statuary, model or design for a work of the fine arts, a photograph of the same.

REQUIREMENTS AS TO PRINTING.

In the case of a book, photograph, chromo, or lithograph, the two copies of the same required to be delivered or deposited as above, must be printed from type set within the limits of the United States, or from plates made therefrom, or from negatives, or drawings on stone made within the limits of the United States, or from transfers made therefrom.

PROVISIONS AS TO IMPORTATION OF COPYRIGHTED WORKS.

During the existence of such copyright the importation into the United States of any book, chromo, lithograph, or photograph, so copyrighted, or any edition or editions thereof, or any plates of the same not made from type set, negatives, or drawings on stone made within the limits of the United States, is prohibited, except in the cases specified in paragraphs 512 to 516, inclusive, in section two of the act entitled, "An Act to reduce the revenue and equalize the duties on imports and for other purposes, approved October 1, 1890 ;" * and except in the case of persons purchasing for use and not for sale, who import subject to the duty thereon, not more than two copies of such book at any one time ; and, except in the case of newspapers and magazines, not containing in whole or in part matter copyrighted under the provisions of this act, unauthorized by the author, which are exempted from prohibition of importation.

In the case of books in foreign languages, of which only translations in English are copyrighted, the prohibition of importation applies only to the translations of the same ; the importation of the books in the original language is permitted.

COPYRIGHTED ARTICLES TO BE MARKED.

No action for the infringement of a copyright can be maintained unless notice of the copyright is given the public by inserting in the several copies of every edition published, on the title page, or the page immediately following, if it be a book; or if a map, chart, musical composition, print, cut, engraving, photograph, painting, drawing, chromo, statue, statuary, or model or design, by inscribing upon some visible portion thereof, or of the substance on which the same shall be mounted, the following words, viz :

" Entered according to Act of Congress, in the year——, by A. B., in the office of the Librarian of Congress, at Washington."

Or, at the option of the owner, the words, "Copyright, 18 —, by A. B."
in either case stating the year the copyright was entered, and the name of the party by whom it was taken out.

A person who shall falsely mark an article as copyrighted is liable to a penalty of one hundred dollars.

APPLICATIONS FOR COPYRIGHT.

An application for copyright protection consists of the following parts:

(*a*) An application for registration, distinctly stating the full name and residence of the claimant, and whether the right is claimed as author, designer, or proprietor. In case an agent is appointed to obtain the registration there should be joined to the application a brief appointment of agent, stating his name and address, and containing a request that all communications relating to said application be addressed to him.

(*b*) A printed copy of the title of the work if it be a book, map, chart, dramatic or musical composition, engraving, cut, print, photograph or chromo, or,

A description of the work if it be a painting, drawing, statue, statuary, or model or design for a work of the fine arts. The printed title required may be a copy of the title page of such publications as have title pages. In other cases, the title must be printed expressly for copyright entry, with name of claimant of copyright. The style of type is immaterial, and the print of a typewriter will be accepted. A separate title is required for each entry, and each title must be printed on paper as large as commercial note (5 ½x8½ inches). The title of a periodical must include the date and number; and each number of a periodical requires a separate entry of copyright.

(*c*) To COMPLETE THE COPYRIGHT. If the article be a book, map, chart, dramatic or musical composition, engraving, cut, print, photograph or chromo, two complete copies of the best edition issued, must be delivered, or deposited in the mail within the United States, addressed to the Librarian of Congress, not later than the day of the publication of such book or other article. And the two copies above required must, as we have already seen, be printed from type set or plates made in the United States, or from negatives or drawings on stone, or transfers therefrom, made within the United States.

In case of a painting, statue, or model or design intended to be perfected as a work of the fine arts, a photograph of the same as large as " cabinet size " (4x6 inches) must be deposited with, or mailed to the Librarian of Congress not later than the day of publication.

Without the deposit of the copies above required the copyright is void, and a penalty of twenty-five dollars is incurred.

The law also requires the deposit of one copy of each new edition wherein any substantial changes are made.

ASSIGNMENTS.

A copyright is assignable in law by any instrument in writing. No particular form of assignment is prescribed. Such assignment must be recorded in the office of the Librarian of Congress within sixty days from its date.

*NOTE.—These paragraphs of the new Tariff act permit free importation of books, etc., more than twenty years old, books in foreign languages, publications imported by the Government, or for societies, colleges, etc., and libraries which have been in use one or more years, brought from abroad by persons or families and not for sale.

FORMS OF DOCUMENTS.

PATENTS.

DOCUMENTS REQUIRED FOR AN APPLICATION FOR PATENT.

(See Body of Book for Detailed Information.)

1. PETITION WITH POWER OF ATTORNEY signed by the inventor. No witnesses nor legalization necessary.
2. SPECIFICATION signed by the inventor and two witnesses. No legalization necessary.
3. OATH signed by the inventor. The oath should be sworn to before a Notary Public or an United States Consular officer having an official seal, and the signature of the officer administering the oath must in all cases be attested by such official seal.
4. DRAWING, if the invention can possibly be illustrated by a drawing. The drawing need not be signed by the inventor, nor legalized in any way.

SPECIAL DIRECTIONS.

Particular attention is called to the following points :

(*a*) The *actual* inventor or inventors *must* sign the Petition and Power of Attorney, the Specification, and the Oath.

(*b*) *Only* the inventor or inventors should so sign. An assignee or other person is not allowed to join with the inventor in making application, and in signing these documents, under any circumstances.

(*c*) The inventor or inventors must, when signing these documents, sign their first, or given name in full, thus : *John Albert Peter Smith*, or *John A. P. Smith*. A document signed J. A. P. Smith, or J. Albert Peter Smith, will be rejected and returned for correction.

(*d*) Careful attention should be paid to the wording of the documents. It is absolutely necessary that they agree in all respects with the forms given below.

(*e*) It is *not sufficient* that the oath be taken before a Commissioner for Administering Affidavits, a Judge, a Justice of the Peace, or other person authorized by law to administer oaths in the country where the deposition is taken. The oath should be made before one of two persons : A Notary Public, or an United States Consular officer, and in either case it is essential that he have an official seal and that it be affixed.

(*f*) The drawing should conform to the rules in all particulars. Lithographs are never accepted. The size of the sheet upon which a drawing is made must be exactly 10 inches wide by 15 inches high. The margin line must be drawn exactly 1 inch from the edge of the sheet. A clear space of at least 1¼ inches must be left at the top of the sheet below the marginal line. The paper should be white.

As a failure to comply with these requirements will insure the rejection of documents, Patent Agents will serve their own interests, and save expense and delays, by seeing that all documents are correctly prepared and executed before they are forwarded for filing.

FORMS FOR APPLICATION BY A SOLE INVENTOR.

PETITION WITH POWER OF ATTORNEY.

To the Commissioner of Patents :

Your petitioner, (*insert full names of inventor*), a citizen, (*or subject, and state of what country applicant is a citizen or subject, as, for instance,* "*a citizen of the Republic of France,*" *or* "*a subject of the Queen of Great Britain and Ireland,*") residing at (*insert residence of applicant*), prays that Letters Patent may be granted to him for the (*insert title of invention*), set forth in the annexed specification ; and he hereby appoints William E. Richards and William W. White, doing business under the name and style of Richards & Co., of the city, county and State of New York, and of Washington, D. C., his attorneys, with full power of substitution and revocation, to prosecute this application, to make alterations and amendments therein, to receive the Patent, and to transact all business in the Patent Office connected therewith. (*Signature.*)

SPECIFICATION.

To all whom it may concern :

Be it known that I, (*insert full name of inventor*), a citizen, (*or subject, and state of what country applicant is a citizen or subject*), and resident of (*insert residence*), have invented a certain new and useful (*insert title of invention and if the invention has already been patented in any other country, insert here the words* for which I have obtained a patent (*or patents*) in and state in what countries patents have been obtained, giving the numbers and dates of the patents, as, "Great Britain No. 1426, bearing date June 24, 1890," etc.,) of which the following is a specification:

The objects of my invention are (*here insert a brief description of the objects of the invention*).

Referring to the drawings which form a part of this specification, Figure 1 is (*here insert a brief description of each figure of the drawings, after which insert the specification or description of the invention, inserting before the claims the words*):

Having now described my invention, what I claim as new and desire to secure by letters patent is:

(*Insert claims*).

In witness whereof I have hereunto set my hand in presence of two witnesses.

(*Inventor signs here.*)

Witnesses :
(*Two Witnesses must sign here.*)

OATH.

(*Insert place of execution.*) .... }
                                                            } ss.
(*Insert name of country.*) .... }

(*Insert name of inventor*), the above-named petitioner, a citizen (*or subject, and state of what country he is a citizen or subject, as for instance, "a citizen of the Republic of Switzerland," or "a subject of the King of Prussia"*), and resident of (*insert residence*), being duly sworn, deposes and says that he verily believes himself to be the original, first, and sole inventor of the (*insert title of invention*) described and claimed in the foregoing specification; that the same has not been patented to himself or to others with his knowledge or consent (*If the invention has not been patented in any other country, add the words* " in any country." *If prior patents exist, add the words* "except in," *and proceed to state the name or names of the country or countries in which it has been patented, and the official number and date of such prior patents, as for example:* "Great Britain, No. 4120, Dated January 1, 1890," etc.,); that the same has not to his knowledge been in public use or on sale in the United States for more than two years prior to this application, and he does not know and does not believe that the same was ever known or used prior to his invention thereof.   (*Signature.*)

Sworn to and subscribed before me }
     this   }
          (*insert date.*)   }   (*Signature of official administering the oath.*)
(*Seal of officer administering oath.*)

FORMS FOR APPLICATION BY JOINT INVENTORS.

PETITION WITH POWER OF ATTORNEY.

To the Commissioner of Patents :

Your petitioners, (*insert name of one inventor*), a citizen (*or subject, and state of what country he is a citizen or subject*), residing at (*insert residence of first inventor*), and (*insert name of second joint inventor*), a citizen (*or subject, and state of what country he is a citizen or subject*), residing at (*insert residence of second inventor*), pray that Letters Patent may be granted to them for the (*insert title of invention*) set forth in the annexed specification : and they hereby appoint William E. Richards and William W. White, doing business under the name and style of Richards & Co., of the city, county and State of New York, and of Washington, D. C., their attorneys, with full power of substitution and revocation to prosecute this application, to make alterations and amendments therein, to receive the Patent, and to transact all business in the Patent Office connected therewith.

(*Signature of first Inventor.*)
(*Signature of second Inventor.*)

SPECIFICATION.

To all whom it may concern :

Be it known that we, (*insert name of one inventor*), a citizen (*or subject, and state of what country he is a citizen or subject*), residing at (*insert his residence*), and (*insert name of second inventor*), a citizen (*or subject, and state of what country he is a citizen or subject*). residing at (*insert his residence*), have invented a certain new and useful (*insert title of invention. If the invention has already been patented in any other country insert here the words* for which we have obtained a patent (*or patents*) in, and state in what countries patents have been obtained, giving the number and date of each patent, as for instance, "Great Britain, No. 1736 bearing date September 22, 1890; France, No. 214,976 bearing date January 1, 1890," etc.*) of which the following is a specification.

The objects of the invention are (*here briefly decribe the objects of the invention*).

Referring to the drawings which form a part of this specification, Figure 1 is (*here give a brief description of each figure of the drawings, and follow with the specification or description of the invention, inserting before the claims the words*):

Having now described our invention, what we claim as new and desire to secure by Letters Patent is:

(*Insert claims.*)

In witness whereof we have hereunto set our hands in presence of two witnesses.

Witnesses: (*First inventor signs here.*)
(*Two witnesses must sign here.*)   (*Second inventor signs here.*)

OATH.

(*Insert place of execution.*) .... }
                                                            } ss.
(*Insert name of country.*) .... }

(*Insert name of one inventor*), a citizen (*or subject, and state of what country he is a citizen or subject*), and resident of (*insert place of residence*), and (*insert name of other inventor*), a citizen (*or subject, and state of what country he is a citizen or subject*), and resident of (*insert place of residence*), the above-named petitioners, being duly sworn, depose and say that they verily believe themselves to be the original, first and joint inventors of the (*insert title of invention*) described and claimed in the foregoing specification; that the same has not been Patented to themselves or to others with their knowledge or consent (*If the invention has not been patented in any other country, add the words* "in any other country." *If prior patents exist, add the words,* "except in," *and proceed to state the name or names of the country or countries in which it has been patented, and the official number and date of such prior patents, as for example:* "*Great Britain, No. 4120, dated January 1, 1800,*" *etc.*); that the same has not to their knowledge been in public use or on sale in the United States for more than two years prior to this application, and they do not know and do not believe that the same was ever known or used prior to their invention thereof.

(*First inventor signs here.*)
(*Second inventor signs here.*)

Sworn to and subscribed before me }
this day of........ (*insert date.*) {
(*Official seal of officer administering oath.*)

(*Signature of official administering oath.*)

FORMS FOR AN APPLICATION BY AN ADMINISTRATOR.

NOTE.—An application by an administrator must be accompanied by a duly certified copy of the letters of administration.

PETITION WITH POWER OF ATTORNEY.

To the Commissioner of Patents:
Your petitioner, (*insert full name*), a citizen (*or subject, and state of what country applicant is a citizen or subject*), residing at (*insert residence*), administrator of the estate of (*insert full name and last residence of inventor*), late a citizen (*or subject, and state of what country he was a citizen or subject*), deceased, as by reference to the duly certified copy of letters of administration hereto annexed will more fully appear, prays that Letters Patent may be granted to him for the invention of the said (*insert name of inventor*), for (*insert title of invention*), set forth in the annexed specification; and he hereby appoints William E. Richards and William W. White, doing business under the name and style of Richards & Co., of the city, county and State of New York, and of Washington, D. C., his attorneys, with full power of substitution and revocation, to prosecute this application, to make alterations and amendments therein, to receive the Patent, and to transact all business in the Patent Office connected therewith.

(*Signature.*)

SPECIFICATION.

To whom it may concern:
Be it known that (*insert name of inventor*), late a citizen of (*or subject of, and proceed to state of what country he was a citizen or subject*), and a resident of (*insert last place of residence*), but now deceased, did invent a certain new and useful (*insert title of invention, and if any foreign patents have been obtained add the words,* for which patents have been obtained in, *and proceed to specify the countries in which patents have been obtained and the number and date of each patent*), of which the following is a full, clear, and exact specification.
The invention has for its object. (*Here proceed with the specification and claims as in other cases.*)

Witnesses:
(*Signatures of two witnesses.*)

(*Signature of administrator*),
Administrator of the estate of (*insert name of deceased inventor*), deceased.

OATH.

(*Insert place of execution.*)........................ }
 }ss.
(*Insert name of country.*)........................ }

(*Insert name of administrator*), the above named petitioner, a citizen (*or subject, and state of what country he is a citizen or subject*), and resident of (*insert residence*), being duly sworn, deposes and says that he is the administrator of the estate of (*insert name of inventor*), late a citizen (*or subject, and state of what country he was a citizen or subject*), and resident of (*insert last place of residence*), deceased; that he verily believes that the said (*insert name of inventor*) was the original, first and sole inventor of the improvement in (*insert title of invention*), described and claimed in the foregoing specification; that the same has not been patented to himself, or to others with his knowledge or consent (*if the invention has not been patented in any country add the words* "in any country." *If prior patents exist, add the words,* "except in the following countries," *and proceed to state the name or names of the country or countries in which the same has been patented, as for example,* "*Great Britain, No. 4125, dated January 1, 1890; France, No. 192,478, dated January 2, 1890,*" *as the case may be*); that the same has not to his knowledge been in public use or on sale in the United States for more than two years prior to this application, and he does not know and does not believe that the same was ever known or used prior to the said (*insert inventor's name*) invention thereof. (*Signature.*)
Sworn and subscribed before me this...........day of...................189.....................
(*Signature of official administering the oath.*)
(*Official seal of officer administering oath.*)

FORMS FOR AN APPLICATION BY AN EXECUTOR.

NOTE.—An application by an executor must be accompanied by a duly certified copy of the letters testamentary.

PETITION WITH POWER OF ATTORNEY.

To the Commissioner of Patents:
Your petitioner, (*insert name and residence of executor*), a citizen (*or subject, and state of what country the executor is a citizen or subject*), executor of the last will and testament of (*insert name and last residence of inventor*), late a citizen (*or subject, and state of what country the inventor was a citizen or subject*), deceased, as by reference to the duly certified copy of letters testamentary, hereto annexed, will more fully appear, prays that Letters Patent may be granted to him for the invention of the said (*insert*

name of inventor), for a (*insert title of invention*), set forth in the annexed specification ; and he hereby appoints William E. Richards, and William W. White, doing business under the name and style of Richards & Co., of the city, county and State of New York, and of Washington, D. C., his attorneys, with full power of substitution and revocation, to prosecute this application, to make alterations and amendments therein, to receive the Patent, and to transact all business in the Patent Office connected therewith.
(Signature.)

SPECIFICATION.

To all whom it may concern :

Be it known that (*insert name of inventor*), who was a citizen of (*or subject of, and state of what country he was a citizen or subject*), and a resident of (*insert last residence*), but is now deceased, did invent a certain new and useful (*insert title of invention, and if any foreign patents have been obtained add the words* for which patents have been obtained in *and proceed to specify the countries in which such patents have been obtained, stating the number and date of each*), of which the following is a full, clear and exact specification.
(Here proceed with the specification and claims as in other cases.)

Witnesses: *(Signature of Executor.)*
(Signatures of two witnesses.)   Executor of the estate of (*insert name of deceased inventor*) deceased.

NOTE.—All the executors, if there be more than one, should join in the application, and in executing the documents.

OATH.

The form is precisely the same as for an administrator, except that he "*deposes and says he is the executor of the last will and testament of*" instead of "administrator of the estate of," in the first few lines of the document.

REVOCATION OF POWER OF ATTORNEY, AND APPOINTMENT OF NEW ATTORNEY.

To the Commissioner of Patents:

The undersigned, having on or about the (*insert date*) appointed (*insert name and address of attorney whose power is to be revoked*), his attorney to prosecute an application for Letters Patents for (*insert title of invention*), which application was filed in the Patent Office on or about (*insert filing date*), serial number (*insert serial number*), hereby revokes the power of attorney then given, and appoints William E. Richards and William W. White, doing business under the name and style of Richards & Co., of the city, county and State of New York, and of Washington, D. C., his attorneys, with full power of substitution and revocation, to prosecute said application, to make alterations and amendments therein, to receive the Patent, and to transact all business in the Patent Office connected therewith.
(Signature.)

FORM FOR SUPPLEMENTAL OATH AS TO FOREIGN PATENTS.

SUPPLEMENTAL OATH AS TO FOREIGN PATENTS.

(Insert place of execution).... .. .. } ss.
(Insert name of country)...................................... }

(Insert name of inventor), whose application for Letters Patent for an improvement in (*insert title of invention*) was filed in the United States Patent Office on or about the (*insert date of filing*), being duly sworn, deposes and says, that he is the applicant named in the application above described ; that he verily believes himself to be the original, first and sole inventor of the said improvements, and that the same have not been patented to him, or to others with his knowledge or consent, except in the following countries: (*here insert the numbers and dates of all existing foreign patents, as for example:* "Great Britain, No. 4715, dated June 4, 1880; France, No. 194,615, dated May 12, 1881," etc., *as the case may be.*)   *(Signature.)*

Sworn to and subscribed before me this (*insert date.*)
(Signature of official administering oath.)
[*Official Seal.*]

FORM OF SUPPLEMENTAL OATH TO ACCOMPANY A NEW OR AN ENLARGED CLAIM.

OATH.

(Insert place of execution)............................... } ss.
(Insert name of country.)............................... }

(Insert name of inventor), whose application for Letters Patent for an improvement in (*insert title of invention*), serial number (*insert serial number*), was filed in the United States Patent Office on or about the (*insert date of filing*), being duly sworn, deposes and says that he verily believes himself to be the original, first and sole inventor of the improvement as described and claimed as follows: (*here insert the claim or claims in question*), in addition to that which was embraced in the claims originally made, and that he does not know and does not believe that the same was ever before known or used, and that the matter sought to be inserted formed a part of his original invention at the date of filing said application, and was invented by him before he filed the same.   *(Signature.)*

Sworn to and subscribed before me this (*insert date.*)
(Signature of official administering the oath.)
[*Official Seal.*]

REISSUES.

FORMS FOR APPLICATION FOR A REISSUE. BY AN INVENTOR.

PETITION WITH POWER OF ATTORNEY.

To the Commissioner of Patents:

Your petitioner, (*insert name of inventor*), a citizen (*or subject, and state of what country the appli-cant is a citizen or subject*), residing at (*insert residence*), prays that he may be allowed to surrender the Letters Patent for an improvement in (*insert title of invention*), granted to him (*insert date of patent*), whereof he is now sole owner (*or, if the patent has been assigned, whereof* (*insert name of assignee*) *on whose behalf and with whose assent this application is made, is now sole owner, by assignment*), and that letters patent may be reissued to him (*or to the said* [*insert name of assignee*]) for the same invention, upon the annexed amended specification. With this petition is filed an abstract of title, duly certified, as required in such cases. And your petitioner hereby appoints William E. Richards and William W. White, doing business under the name and style of Richards & Co., of the city, county and State of New York, and of Washington, D. C., his attorneys, with full power of substitution and revocation, to prosecute this application, to make alterations and amendments therein, to receive the Patent, and to transact all business in the Patent Office connected therewith.   (*Signature.*)

NOTE.—If the patent has been assigned, the assent of the assignee must be procured in the following form :

The undersigned, assignee of the entire (*or if of an interest, here define it*) interest in the above mentioned letters patent, hereby assents to the accompanying application.
(*Signature of assignee.*)

OATH.

(*Insert place of execution*)........................)

                                                    }- ss.

(*Insert name of country*).........................)

(*Insert name of inventor*), the above-named petitioner, being duly sworn, deposes and says that he does verily believe himself to be the original and first inventor of the improvement set forth and claimed in the foregoing specification, and for which improvement he solicits a patent ; that deponent does not know and does not believe that said improvement was ever before known or used ; that deponent is a citizen (*or subject, and state of what country he is a citizen or subject*), and resides at (*insert residence*) ; that deponent verily believes that the letters patent referred to in the foregoing petition and specification, and herewith surrendered, are inoperative (*or invalid*) for the reason that the specification thereof is de-fective (*or insufficient*), and that such defect (*or insufficiency*) consists particularly in (*here insert a state-ment particularly specifying such defects or insufficiencies*) ; and deponent further says that the errors which render such patent so inoperative (*or invalid*) arose from inadvertence (*or accident, or mistake*), and without any fraudulent or deceptive intention on the part of deponent ; that the following is a true specification of the errors which it is claimed constitute such inadvertence (*or accident, or mistake*), relied upon : (*here recite the facts*) ; that such errors so particularly specified arose (*or occurred*) as follows : (*state here how the errors arose or occurred*).   (*Signature of Inventor.*)
Subscribed and sworn to before me this (*insert date*).

                                                    (*Signature of official administering oath.*)

    [*Official Seal.*]

FORMS FOR APPLICATION FOR RE-ISSUE. BY THE ASSIGNEES.

(*To be used only when the inventor is dead.*)

PETITION WITH POWER OF ATTORNEY FOR A RE-ISSUE.

To the Commissioner of Patents :

Your petitioners, (*insert name of one assignee*), a citizen (*or subject, and state of what country he is a citizen or subject*), residing at (*insert place of residence*), and (*insert name of other assignee*), a citizen (*or subject, and state of what country he is a citizen or subject*), residing at (*insert place of residence*), pray that they may be allowed to surrender the Letters Patent for an improvement in (*insert title of invention*), granted (*insert date of patent*), to (*insert name of patentee*), now deceased, whereof they are now owners by assignment of the entire interest, and that the Letters Patent may be reissued to them for the same in-vention, upon the annexed amended specification. With this petition is filed an abstract of title, duly certified, as required in such cases. Your petitioners hereby appoint William E. Richards and William W. White, doing business under the name and style of Richards & Co., of the city, county and State of New York, and of Washington, D. C., their attorneys, with full powers of substitution and revocation, to prosecute this application, to make alterations and amendments therein, to receive the Patent, and to transact all business in the Patent Office connected therewith.   (*Signatures.*)

OATH.

(*Insert place of execution*).........................)

                                                    }- ss.

(*Insert name of country*) .. ..)

(*Insert names, addresses, and citizenship of assignees*), the above named petitioners, being duly sworn, depose and say that they verily believe that the aforesaid letters patent granted to (*insert name of paten-tee*) are (*here follow allegations as in oath for reissue by inventor, the necessary changes being made to make them apply to the assignees, after which and before the signatures the following must be added*): that the entire title to said letters patent is vested in them, and that they verily believe the said (*insert name of patentee*) to be the first and original inventor of the invention set forth and claimed in the fore-going amended specification, and that the said (*insert name of patentee*) is now deceased.
                                                    (*Signatures of assignees.*)
Sworn to and subscribed before me this (*insert date*).
                                                    (*Signature of official administering oath.*)
    [*Official Seal.*]

DISCLAIMER.

FORM FOR DISCLAIMER AFTER ISSUE OF PATENT.

DISCLAIMER.

To the Commissioner of Patents:

Your petitioner, (*insert name of disclaimant*), a citizen (*or subject, and state of what country he is a citizen or subject*), residing at (*insert residence*), represents that in the matter of a certain improvement in (*insert title of invention*), for which letters patent of the United States No. (*insert number of patent*) were granted to (*insert name of patentee*) on the (*insert date of patent*), he is the (*here set forth the exact facts as to the interests in said patent owned by the disclaimant: if he is the assignee, state the liber and page where assignment is recorded*), and that he has reason to believe that through inadvertence (*or accident or mistake*) the specification and claim of said letters patent are too broad, including that of which the patentee was not the first inventor. Your petitioner, therefore, hereby enters his disclaimer to that part of the claim in said specification which is in the following words, to wit: (*here recite the part disclaimed.*)

(*Signature.*)

Witness:
(*Signature of Witness.*)

INTERFERENCE.

FORM OF PRELIMINARY STATEMENT IN INTERFERENCE FOR A FOREIGN INVENTOR.

STATEMENT IN INTERFERENCE.

(*Preliminary Statement of Foreign Inventor.*)

Interference in United States Patent Office }
    No. .... }
  Preliminary Statement of }
  (*Insert name of inventor.*) }

(*Insert name and residence of inventor*), being duly sworn, doth depose and say that he is a party to the interference declared by the Commissioner of Patents (*insert date of the declaration of interference*), between his application for patent filed (*insert date of filing*), serial number (*insert serial number*), and the (*state whether application or patent*) of (*insert name of opponent*), No. (*insert number*), for (*insert title of invention*); that he made the invention set forth in the declaration of interference, being at that time in (*insert name of place*); that patents for such invention were applied for and obtained as follows: (*here insert the dates of all applications for foreign patents that have been made, together with the numbers and dates of each patent, as for instance: "Application filed in Great Britain, December 4th, 1888, patent numbered 24,076 of 1888, and dated December 4th, 1888," etc., etc. If a patent has not been obtained in any country it should be so stated.*)

That such invention was fully described in: (*Here set forth any publications of the invention, giving the dates, and stating where such publications appeared, and when and where such publications were introduced into the United States, if at all. If the invention was never described in a publication it should be so stated.*)

That knowledge of such invention was introduced into the United States under the following circumstances: On (*insert date*), the said (*name of inventor*) wrote a letter to (*insert name*), residing at (*insert residence*), describing such invention, and soliciting his services in procuring a patent therefor in the United States. '*Here proceed to recite the facts, showing to whom in the United States knowledge of the invention was disclosed for the purpose of making application for patent therefor; the earliest date upon which such knowledge of the invention was introduced into the United States, etc.*

If the invention has been manufactured in the United States, state when, and to whom the applicant first wrote to secure such manufacture, and also whether the invention has been described in trade circulars in the United States, the date, etc., and any other information that will show when and where the invention was first introduced into or disclosed in the United States. If the invention has not been introduced into the United States otherwise than by the application papers, it should be so stated.)

(*Signature.*)

Subscribed and sworn to before me this (*insert date*).

(*Signature of Official administering oath.*)

[*Official Seal.*]

NOTE.—This statement must be subscribed and sworn (or affirmed) to before a Notary Public, or a Diplomatic or Consular Officer of the United States, who must in all cases affix his official seal.

ASSIGNMENTS.

FORM OF ASSIGNMENT TO ACCOMPANY AN APPLICATION FOR PATENT WHEN IT IS DESIRED THAT THE PATENT SHALL ISSUE TO AN ASSIGNEE.

ASSIGNMENT.

Whereas I, (*insert name of inventor*), of (*insert residence of inventor*), have invented a certain new and useful (*insert title of invention*), for which I am about to make application for letters patent of the United States therefor.

And Whereas, (*insert name of assignee*), of (*insert residence of assignee*), is desirous of acquiring an interest in said invention, and in the letters patent to be obtained therefor;

Now, therefore, to all whom it may concern, be it known that for and in consideration of the sum of (*insert consideration*), to me in hand paid, the receipt of which is hereby acknowledged, I, the said (*insert name of assignor*), have sold, assigned, and transferred, and by these presents do sell, assign, and transfer unto the said (*insert name of assignee*), all my right, title and interest in and to the said invention, as fully set forth and described in the specification prepared and executed by me on the (*insert date of execution of application*), preparatory to obtaining letters patent of the United States therefor : and I do hereby authorize and request the Commissioner of Patents to issue the said letters patent when granted to the said (*insert name of assignee*).

In testimony whereof I have hereunto set my hand and affixed my seal this (*insert date*).

(*Signature of Inventor.*)   [SEAL.]

In presence of
(*Signatures of two witnesses.*)

FORM OF ASSIGNMENT OF PARTIAL INTEREST, WHERE APPLICATION HAS BEEN FILED, WITH REQUEST TO ISSUE PATENT TO INVENTOR AND ASSIGNEE JOINTLY.

ASSIGNMENT.

Whereas I, (*insert name of inventor*), of (*insert residence of inventor*), have invented a certain new and useful (*insert title of invention*), for which I have made application for letters patent of the United States therefor, said application having been filed in the United States Patent Office on or about (*insert date upon which application was filed*), serial number (*insert serial number of application*).

And Whereas, (*insert name of assignee*), of (*insert residence of assignee*), is desirous of acquiring an interest in said invention, and in the letters patent to be obtained therefor :

Now, therefore, to all whom it may concern, be it known, that for and in consideration of the sum of (*insert consideration*), to me in hand paid, the receipt of which is hereby acknowledged, I, the said (*insert name of inventor*), have sold, assigned, and transferred, and by these presents do sell, assign, and transfer unto the said (*insert name of assignee*), an undivided one-half part of the whole right, title and interest in and to the said invention, and in and to the letters patent to be obtained therefor, and I do hereby authorize and request the Commissioner of Patents to issue the said letters patent when granted to me and to the said (*insert name of assignee*), jointly.

In testimony whereof I have hereunto set my hand and affixed my seal this (*insert date*), at (*insert place of execution*).

In presence of
(*Signatures of two witnesses.*)   (*Signature.*)   [SEAL.]

FORM OF ASSIGNMENT, AFTER ISSUE OF PATENT.

ASSIGNMENT.

Whereas I, (*insert name and address of patentee*), did obtain letters patent of the United States of America, for an invention entitled (*insert title of invention*), which letters patent are numbered (*insert number of patent*), and bear date the (*insert date of patent*).

And Whereas, (*insert name and address of assignee*), is desirous of acquiring an interest in the same :

Now, Therefore, to all whom it may concern, be it known that for and in consideration of the sum of (*insert consideration*), to me in hand paid, the receipt of which is hereby acknowledged, I, the said (*insert name of assignor*), have sold, assigned, and transferred, and by these present do sell, assign and transfer unto the said (*insert name of assignee*), all my right, title, and interest (*or an undivided one-half interest, or whatever interest may be assigned, as the case may be*), in and to the said invention ,and in and to the letters patent therefor aforesaid: the same to be held and enjoyed by the said (*insert name of assignee*), for his own use and behoof, and for the use and behoof of his legal representatives and assigns, to the full end of the term for which said letters patent are or may be granted, as fully and entirely as the same would have been held and enjoyed by me had this assignment and sale not have been made.

In testimony whereof I have hereunto set my hand and affixed my seal at (*insert place of execution*), this (*insert date*).

In presence of
(*Signatures of two witnesses.*)   (*Signature.*)   [SEAL.]

CAVEATS.

(See body of book for detailed information.)

NOTE.—Only citizens of the United States, or aliens who have resided in the United States for one year next preceding the filing of the caveat, and who have declared their intention to become citizens of the United States, are entitled to file caveats.

FORM OF PETITION WITH POWER OF ATTORNEY.

To the Commissioner of Patents :

The petition of (*insert name of petitioner*), a citizen of the United States (*or if a resident alien recite the facts in accordance with the above note*), residing at (*insert residence*), represents :

That he has made certain improvements in (*insert title of invention*), and that he is now engaged in making experiments for the purpose of perfecting the same, preparatory to applying for letters patent therefor. He therefore prays that the subjoined description of his invention may be filed as a caveat in the confidential archives of the Patent Office.

And he hereby appoints William E. Richards and William W. White, doing business under the name and style of Richards & Co., of the city, county and State of New York, and of Washington, D. C., his attorneys, with full power of substitution and revocation, to prosecute this application, to make alterations and amendments therein, and to transact all business in the Patent Office connected therewith.

(*Signature.*)

SPECIFICATION.

To the Commissioner of Patents :

Be it known that I, (*insert name of caveator*), a citizen of the United States (*or if a resident alien recite the facts in accordance with the above note*), and residing at (*insert residence*), having invented (*insert title of invention*), and desiring further to mature the same, file this my caveat therefor, and pray protection of my right until I shall have matured my invention.

The following is a description of my invention, which is as full, clear, and exact as I am able at this time to give, reference being had to the drawing hereto annexed.

(*Here insert a description of the invention. It is not necessary to append claims to a caveat.*)

Witnesses :   (*Signature of Caveator.*)
(*Signatures of two witnesses.*)

OATH.

(Insert place of execution).......... .... }
                                                      } ss.
(Insert name of country).........................

    (Insert name of caveator), the above named petitioner, a citizen of the United States *(or if a resident alien recite the facts in accordance with above note)*, and resident of *(insert residence)*, being duly sworn, deposes and says that he verily believes himself to be the original and first inventor of the *(insert title of invention)*, described in the foregoing specification.   *(Signature of Caveator.)*
    Sworn to and subscribed before me this *(insert date)*.

                                     (Signature of official administering oath.)
    [*Official Seal.*]

DESIGN PATENTS.
(See body of book for detailed information.)
DOCUMENTS REQUIRED.

    The documents required are the same as for other Patents. The forms for Specifications and Oaths are the same as for other patents, except that in reciting the title of the invention the words "a new and original design for" are to precede the title. The petition must state the term for which protection is asked, as follows:

FORM OF PETITION FOR DESIGN PATENT.

To the Commissioner of Patents:
    Your petitioner, *(insert name of inventor)*, a citizen of *(or subject of, and state of what country he is a citizen or subject)*, residing at *(insert residence)*. prays that letters patent may be granted to him for the term of *(here insert the term asked for, whether three and one-half, seven, or fourteen years)*, for the new and original design for *(insert title of invention)*, set forth in the annexed specification, and he hereby appoints William E. Richards and William W. White, doing business under the name and style of Richards & Co., of the city, county and State of New York, and of Washington, D. C., his attorneys, with full power of substitution and revocation, to prosecute this application, to make alterations and amendments therein, to sign the drawings, to receive the Patent, and to transact all business in the Patent Office connected therewith.   *(Signature of Inventor.)*

TRADE MARKS.
(See body of book for detailed information.)

DOCUMENTS REQUIRED FOR AN APPLICATION.

    1. LETTER OF ADVICE AND POWER OF ATTORNEY signed by the owner of the trade mark. No witnesses or legalization required.
    2. STATEMENT or specification of the trade mark, signed by the owner of the trade mark and two witnesses. No legalization required.
    3. DECLARATION signed and sworn to by the owner of the trade mark if the owner be an individual; by a member of the firm, if the owner be a firm; by an officer of the corporation, if the owner be a corporation. The oath must be sworn to before a Notary Public or a Consular Officer of the United States, who must in all cases affix his official seal.
    4. A DRAWING, made in accordance with the rules prescribed for drawings for mechanical patents. If for any reason the drawing does not satisfactorily illustrate the trade mark, three or more fac-similes of the trade mark as it is actually used should be forwarded with the drawing. These need not be signed or legalized in any way. Only two such fac-similes are required to be filed in the Patent Office, but at least one additional copy, and preferably more, should be forwarded for our use in prosecuting the application.

SPECIAL DIRECTIONS.

    Delays and expense will be avoided if Patent Agents will see that their applications conform to the rules in the following particulars:
    1. The statement or specification of the trade mark must state the date since when the trade mark has been used continuously by the applicant; the class of merchandise to which it is appropriated, as well as the particular goods on which it is used, and how applied.
    2. The declaration must name one or more foreign nations or Indian tribes between which and the United States the trade mark is used.
    3. The drawing furnished must comply in all respects with the rules prescribed for drawings for patents. The fac-similes sent should all be alike, and should be upon flexible paper.
    4. If the applicant be a firm, the name of the firm should be signed to the Letter of Advice and the Statement, but the Declaration should be signed by a member of the firm, for the firm.
    5. If the applicant be a corporation, the name of the corporation should be signed to the Letter of Advice, and the Statement, but the Declaration should be signed by one of the principal officers of the Corporation in his own name, stating his title of office. The seal of the Corporation should be affixed to authenticate his signature.

FORMS FOR APPLICATION. BY AN INDIVIDUAL.

APPLICATION FOR THE REGISTRATION OF A TRADE MARK.

LETTER OF ADVICE WITH POWER OF ATTORNEY.

To the Commissioner of Patents:

The undersigned presents herewith a fac-simile of his lawful trade mark and requests that the same, together with the accompanying statement and declaration, may be registered in the United States Patent Office, in accordance with the law in such cases made and provided; and he hereby appoints William E. Richards and William W. White, doing business under the name and style of Richards & Co., of the city, county and State of New York, and of Washington, D. C., his attorneys, with full power of substitution and revocation, to prosecute this application, to make alterations and amendments therein, to receive the Certificate of Registration, and to transact all business in the Patent Office connected therewith. *(Signature.)*

STATEMENT.

To all whom it may concern:

Be it known that I. *(insert name of applicant)*, a citizen of *(or subject of, and state of what country he is a citizen or subject)*, residing at *(insert residence)*, and doing business at *(insert business address, naming street and number)*, have adopted for my use a trade mark for *(insert name of goods upon which trade mark is used)*, of which the following is a full, clear and exact specification:

My trade mark consists of *(state of what the trade mark consists)*. This has generally been arranged as shown in the accompanying fac-simile, which represents *(here insert a complete description of the trade mark, describing in detail all of its parts and features)*.

The essential feature of my trade mark is *(here name the essential features of the trade mark claimed)*. This trade mark I have used continuously in my business since *(insert date since when the trade mark has been continuously used)*. The class of merchandise to which this trade mark is appropriated is *(here name such class)*, and the particular description of goods comprised in said class upon which I use it is *(here name the particular goods or commodities upon which it is used)*. It is my practice to apply my trade mark by *(here state the manner in which the trade mark is applied)*.

In witness whereof I have hereunto set my hand in presence of two witnesses.

(Signature.)

Witnesses:

(Signatures of two Witnesses.)

DECLARATION.

(Insert place of execution.) .... ⎫
⎬ *ss.*
(Insert name of country.) .... ⎭

(Insert name of applicant), being duly sworn, deposes and says that he is the applicant named in the foregoing statement; that he verily believes that the foregoing statement is true; that he has at this time a right to the use of the trade mark therein described; that no other person, firm or corporation has the right to such use, either in the identical form or in any such near resemblance thereto as might be calculated to deceive; that it is used by him in commerce between the United States and foreign nations or Indian tribes, and particularly with *(here name one or more foreign countries or Indian tribes or both, between which and the United States it is used in commerce)*; and that the description and fac-similes presented for record truly represent the trade mark sought to be registered.

(Signature.)

Sworn and subscribed before me, a *(insert title of officer before whom the declaration is made)*, this *(insert date)*.

(Signature of official administering oath.)

[*Official Seal.*]

FORMS FOR APPLICATION. BY A FIRM.

APPLICATION FOR THE REGISTRATION OF A TRADE MARK.

LETTER OF ADVICE WITH POWER OF ATTORNEY.

To the Commissioner of Patents:

The undersigned present herewith a fac-simile of their lawful trade mark and request that the same, together with the accompanying statement and declaration, may be registered in the United States Patent Office, in accordance with the law in such cases made and provided; and they hereby appoint William E. Richards and William W. White, doing business under the name and style of Richards & Co., of the city, county and State of New York, and of Washington, D. C., their attorneys, with full power of substitution and revocation, to prosecute this application, to make alterations and amendments therein, to receive the Certificate of Registration, and to transact all business in the Patent Office connected therewith. *(Signature of Firm.)*

STATEMENT.

To all whom it may concern:

Be it known that we, *(insert name of firm)*, a firm domiciled in *(state place of domicile)*, and doing business at *(insert business address, naming street and number)*, have adopted for our use a trade mark for *(here insert name of goods upon which the trade mark is used)*, of which the following is a full, clear, and exact specification:

Our trade mark consists of *(state of what the trade mark consists)*. This has generally been arranged as shown in the accompanying fac-simile, which represents *(here insert a complete description of the trade mark, describing in detail all of its parts and features)*.

The essential feature of our trade mark is *(here name the essential features claimed)*.

This trade mark has been used continuously in business by us and those from whom we derive our title since *(insert date since when the trade mark has been continuously used)*. The class of merchandise to which this trade mark is appropriated is (*here name such class*), and the particular description of goods comprised in such class on which it is used by us is (*here name the particular goods or commodities upon which it is used*). It has been our practice to apply our trade mark by (*here state the manner in which the trade mark is applied*).

In witness whereof we have hereunto set our hands in presence of two witnesses.

(*Signature of Firm.*)

Witnesses :
(*Signatures of two witnesses.*)

DECLARATION.

(*Insert place of execution.*)........................ ⎫
⎬ ss.
(*Insert name of country.*)......................... ⎭

(*Insert the name of the member of the firm who makes the declaration*), being duly sworn, deposes and says that he is a member of the firm, the applicant named in the foregoing statement; that he verily believes that the foregoing statement is true; that the said firm has at this time a right to the use of the trade mark therein described; that no other person, firm, or corporation has the right to such use, either in the identical form or in any such near resemblance thereto as might be calculated to deceive; that the trade mark is used by the said firm in commerce between the United States and foreign nations or Indian tribes, and particularly with (*here name one or more foreign nations or Indian tribes or both, between which and the United States it is used in commerce*), and that the description and fac-similes presented for record truly represent the trade mark sought to be registered.

(*Signature of the member of the firm who makes the declaration.*)

Sworn and subscribed before me, a (*state official* ⎫
title of officer administering oath.) ⎬
this (*insert date.*) ⎭

[*Official Seal.*] (*Signature of official administering oath.*)

FORM OF APPLICATION. BY A CORPORATION.

APPLICATION FOR THE REGISTRATION OF A TRADE MARK.

LETTER OF ADVICE WITH POWER OF ATTORNEY.

To the Commissioner of Patents :

The undersigned presents herewith a fac-simile of its lawful trade mark and requests that the same, together with the accompanying statement and declaration, may be registered in the United States Patent Office, in accordance with the law in such cases made and provided ; and it hereby appoints William E. Richards and William W. White, doing business under the name and style of Richards & Co., of the city, county and State of New York, and of Washington, D. C., its attorneys, with full power of substitution and revocation, to prosecute this application, to make alterations and amendments therein, to receive the Certificate of Registration, and to transact all business in the Patent Office connected therewith.

(*Signature of Corporation.*)

STATEMENT.

To all whom it may concern :

Be it known that the (*insert name of corporation*), a corporation organized under the laws of (*state under what laws the corporation is organized*), and located in (*state where located*), and doing business in (*state business address of corporation, giving street and number*), has adopted for its use a trade mark for (*state goods upon which trade mark is used*), of which the following is a full, clear and exact specification :

The trade mark of said company consists of (*state of what the trade mark consists*). This has generally been arranged as shown in the accompanying fac-simile, in which (*here insert a complete description of the trade mark, describing in detail all of its parts and features*).

The essential features of the said trade mark are (*here name the essential features claimed*).

This trade mark has been continuously used by said corporation since (*state date since when the trade mark has been continuously used*). The class of merchandise to which this trade mark is applied is (*state class*), and the particular description of goods comprised in such class on which it is used by the said company is (*here name the goods or commodities upon which it is used*). It is usually (*here state how the trade mark is applied or affixed.*)

(*Signature of Corporation.*)

Witnesses : By (*Signature of official signing same.*)
(*Signatures of two witnesses.*) (*Title of official who signed.*)
[*Seal of Corporation.*]

DECLARATION.

(*Insert place of execution*)........................... ⎫
⎬ ss.
(*Insert name of country*)............................. ⎭

(*Insert name of the officer of the corporation who makes the declaration*), being duly sworn, deposes and says that he is (*state his title of office*) of the corporation, the applicant named in the foregoing statement; that he verily believes that the foregoing statement is true; that the said corporation has at this time a right to the use of the trade mark therein described; that no other person, firm or corporation has the right to such use, either in the identical form or in any such near resemblance thereto as might be calculated to deceive ; that the trade mark is used by said corporation in commerce between the United States and foreign nations or Indian tribes, and particularly with (*here name one or more foreign nations or Indian tribes or both, between which and the United States the trade mark is used in commerce*), and that the description and fac-similes presented for record truly represent the trade mark sought to be registered.

(*Signature of the officer of the corporation who makes the declaration.*)

[*Seal of Corporation.*]

Sworn and subscribed before me, a (*state official* ⎫
title of the person administering the oath)........ ⎬
..............this (*insert date*).................... ⎭
[*Official Seal.*]

(*Signature of official administering oath.*)

LABELS AND PRINTS.

(See body of book for detailed information.)

DOCUMENTS REQUIRED FOR APPLICATIONS.

1. APPLICATION FOR REGISTRATION signed by the owner of the label or print. No witnesses or legalization required.

2. SIX COPIES OF THE LABEL OR PRINT. These need not be signed or legalized in any way. The Patent Office only requires five copies, but at least one additional copy should be furnished for our own use in prosecuting the application.

FORM OF APPLICATION. BY AN INDIVIDUAL.

To the Commissioner of Patents:
The undersigned, *(insert name of applicant)*, of *(insert residence)*, and a citizen of *(or subject of, and state of what country he is a citizen or subject)*, hereby furnishes five copies of a label *(or print, as the case may be)*, to be used for *(state use of label or print)*, of which he is the sole proprietor. The title of said label *(or print)* is *(insert title)*, and the said label *(or print)* consists of the words and figures as follows, to wit: *(here insert a full description of the label or print)*.
And he hereby requests that the said label *(or print)* be registered in the Patent Office, in accordance with the Act of Congress to that effect, approved June 18, 1874.
And he hereby appoints William E. Richards and William W. White, doing business under the name and style of Richards & Co., of the city, county and State of New York, and of Washington, D. C., his attorneys, with full powers of substitution and revocation, to prosecute this application, to make alterations and amendments therein, to receive the Certificate of Registration, and to transact all business in the Patent Office connected therewith.

(Insert place and date of execution).

(Signature.)
Proprietor.

FORM OF APPLICATION. BY A FIRM.

To the Commissioner of Patents:
The undersigned, *(insert name of firm)*, a firm domiciled in *(insert domicile)*, and doing business at *(insert business address, giving street and number)*, hereby furnishes five copies of a label *(or print, as the case may be)*, to be used for *(state use of label or print)*, of which they are the sole proprietors. The title of said label *(or print)* is *(insert title)*, and the said label *(or print)* consists of the words and figures as follows, to wit:—*(here insert a full description of the label or print)*.
And they hereby request that the said label *(or print)* be registered in the Patent Office, in accordance with the Act of Congress to that effect, approved June 18, 1874.
And they hereby appoint *(insert power of attorney in the same form as given above, in form of application by an individual)*.

(Place and date of execution.)

(Signature of firm).
Proprietors.

FORM OF APPLICATION. BY A CORPORATION.

To the Commissioner of Patents:
The applicant, a corporation created by authority of the laws of *(state under what law corporation was organized)*, and doing business at *(insert business address, giving street and number, city and country)*, hereby furnishes five copies of a label *(or print, as the case may be)*, to be used for *(state use of label or print)*, of which it is the sole proprietor. The title of said label *(or print)* is *(insert title)*, and the said label *(or print)* consists of the words and figures as follows, to wit; *(here insert description of label or print)*.
And it is hereby requested that the said label *(or print)* be registered in the Patent Office, in accordance with the Act of Congress to that effect, approved June 18, 1874.
And it hereby appoints *(insert power of attorney in the same form as given above, in form of application by an individual)*.
(Place and date of execution.)

(Signature of corporation.)
By *(signature of official signing same.)*
(Title of official signing.)

[*Seal of corporation.*]

COPYRIGHTS.

(See body of book for detailed information.)

DOCUMENTS REQUIRED FOR APPLICATION.

1. APPLICATION FOR REGISTRATION, signed by the applicant. No witnesses or legalization required.

2. TWO PRINTED COPIES OF THE TITLE OF THE BOOK. No signatures or legalization required. Only one copy is required to be filed with the Librarian, but we should be furnished with at least one additional copy for use in our office.

FORM OF APPLICATION.

To the Librarian of Congress, Washington, D. C.:
The undersigned, *(insert name of applicant)*, a citizen of *(or subject of, and state of what country he is a citizen or subject)*, and resident of *(insert residence)*, presents herewith a printed copy of the title of a *(state whether a book, map, chart, dramatic or musical composition, or whatever the work may be)*, for which he desires copyright protection in accordance with the law in such cases made and provided.

He claims the right to such copyright protection as the *(state whether he claims as author, designer, or proprietor)* of the work, the printed title of which is presented herewith, and he hereby appoints William E. Richards and William W. White, doing business under the name and style of Richards & Co., of the city, county and State of New York, and of Washington, D. C., his attorneys, with full powers of substitution and revocation, to prosecute this application, to pay all fees required by law, to receive the Certificate of Registration, and to transact all business relating thereto.

(Signature.)

(Place and date of execution.)

TO COMPLETE THE COPYRIGHT.

THREE COPIES OF THE WORK should be furnished us in sufficient time so that we may file the copies required by law at a day *not later than the day of publication in any country.* Only two copies are required to be filed with the Librarian, but we would request that at least one additional copy be furnished us for our use and to complete our files.

SCHEDULE OF GOVERNMENT FEES.

All fees payable are required to be paid in advance—that is, upon making any application for any action for which a fee is payable.

PATENTS AND DESIGN PATENTS.

The following is the schedule of fees and of prices of publications, etc., of the Patent Office:

On filing each original application for a design patent for three years and six months............ $10 00
On filing each original application for a design patent for seven years........................... 15 00
On filing each original application for a design patent for fourteen years........................ 30 00
On allowance of an application for a design patent, no further charge.
On filing each caveat.. 10 00
On filing each original application for a patent.................................... 15 00
On allowance of an original application for a patent, except in design cases....... 20 00
On filing disclaimer... 10 00
On filing every application for the reissue of a patent............................ 30 00
On filing each application for a division of a reissue............................. 30 00
On allowance of an application for the reissue of a patent, no further charge.
On filing every application for an extension of a patent........................... 50 00
On the granting of every extension of a patent.................................... 50 00
On filing an appeal for the first time from a primary examiner or the examiner of interferences to the examiners-in-chief.. 10 00
On filing every appeal from the examiners-in-chief to the Commissioner............. 20 00
For manuscript copies of records in the English language, for every one hundred words or fraction thereof... 10
If certified, for the certificate, additional...................................... 25
For copies of drawings not in print, the reasonable cost of making them.
For uncertified copies of the specifications and accompanying drawings of all patents which are printed, per copy.. 10
For twenty coupon orders, each coupon good until used for one copy of a printed specification and drawing.. 2 00
For certified copies of printed patents:
For specification and drawing, per copy... 10
For the certificate... 25
For the grant... 50
For the specification, if not in print, for every one hundred words or fraction thereof............ 10
For the drawings, if in print... 10
For the drawings, if not in print, the reasonable cost of making them
For certifying to a duplicate of a model.. 50
For abstracts of title to patents or inventions:
For the certificate of search... 1 00
For each brief from the digest of assignments..................................... 20
For copies of matter in any foreign language, for every one hundred words or a fraction thereof.. 20
For translation, for every one hundred words or fraction thereof.................. 50
For recording every assignment, agreement, power of attorney, or other paper, of three hundred words or under... 1 00
For recording every assignment, agreement, power of attorney, or other paper of over three hundred words and under one thousand words.. 2 00
For recording every assignment, agreement, power of attorney, or other paper of over one thousand words... 3 00
For assistance to attorneys and others in the examination of records, one hour or less........... 50
For each additional hour or fraction thereof...................................... 50
For assistance to attorneys in the examination of patents or other matter in the scientific library, one hour or less... 1 00
Each additional hour or fraction thereof.. 1 00
For subscription to the Official Gazette, published every Tuesday, all subscriptions to commence with the beginning of a volume, none being taken for a less period than three months, and there being no club rates or discount to newsdealers, as follows: To all subscribers within the United States and Canada, one year.. 5 00
To foreign subscribers, except in Canada.. 7 00
Single numbers.. 10
For bound volumes of the Official Gazette:
Semi-annual volumes, from January 1, 1872, to June 30, 1883, full sheep binding, per volume. 4 00
Semi-annual volumes, from January 1, 1872, to June 30, 1883, half sheep binding, per volume... 3 50
Quarterly volumes subsequent to July 1, 1883, full sheep binding, per volume............. 2 75

For the annual index—lists of patentees and inventions, alphabetically arranged, with date of patent, number, etc., from January, 1872—one volume each year, full law binding, per volume... 2 00
In paper covers, per volume.. 1 00
For the general index—a list of inventions patented from 1790 to 1873, with the name of inventor, residence, date of patent, number, etc.—three volumes full law binding, per set............... 10 00
For the index from 1790 to 1836—a list of inventions patented from 1790 to 1836, photolithographed from Patent Office Reports—one volume, full law binding.................................... 5 00
For the monthly volumes, containing the specifications and photolithographed copies of the drawings of all patents issued during the month, certified, bound full sheep, per volume............. 12 00
For the monthly volumes, containing the specifications and photolithographed copies of the drawings of all patents issued during the month, certified, bound half sheep, per volume.......... 10 00
For the index to patents relating to electricity, granted by the United States prior to June 30, 1882, one volume, two hundred and fifty pages, bound.....................................$........ 5 00
In paper covers... 3 00
Annual appendixes for each fiscal year subsequent to June 30, 1882, paper covers.................. 1 50
For Commissioners' Decisions :
    For 1869-'70-'71, bound in one volume, full law binding..................................... 2 00
    For 1872-'73-'74, bound in one volume, full law binding..................................... 2 00
    For 1875-'76, bound in one volume, with decisions of United States courts in patent cases, full law binding.. 2 00
    For 1875-'76, bound in paper covers... 1 00
    For 1877-'78-'79-'80-'81-'82.'83, one volume *each year*, with decisions of United States courts, full law binding, per volume... 2 00
    For 1877-'78-'79-'80-'81-'82-'83, bound in paper covers...................................... 1 00
    Pamphlet of the Rules of Practice.. Free

TRADE MARKS AND LABELS.

On filing an application for registration of a trade mark.. $25 00
On filing an application for registration of a label.. 6 00
For assignments, copies of records, etc., the same as for patents..............................

COPYRIGHTS.

For recording each copyright for citizens or residents of the United States...................... $0 50
For recording each copyright for an alien.. 1 00
For certificate of copyright... 50
For recording an assignment... 1 00
For a certified copy of any record of assignment.. 1 00
For a copy of the record of any copyright entry... 1 00

www.ingramcontent.com/pod-product-compliance
Lightning Source LLC
Chambersburg PA
CBHW031221290326
41931CB00036B/1331